HOLT SCIENCE & TECHNOLOGY

Sound and Light

HOLT, RINEHART AND WINSTON

A Harcourt Classroom Education Company

Austin · New York · Orlando · Atlanta · San Francisco · Boston · Dallas · Toronto · London

Staff Credits

Editorial

Robert W. Todd, Executive Editor

Anne Earvolino, Senior Editor

Michael Mazza, Ken Shepardson, Kelly Rizk, Bill Burnside, Editors

ANCILLARIES

Jennifer Childers, Senior Editor

Chris Colby, Molly Frohlich, Shari Husain, Kristen McCardel, Sabelyn Pussman, Erin Roberson

COPYEDITING

Dawn Spinozza, Copyediting Supervisor

EDITORIAL SUPPORT STAFF

Jeanne Graham, Mary Helbling, Tanu'e White, Doug Rutley

EDITORIAL PERMISSIONS

Cathy Paré, Permissions Manager

Jan Harrington, Permissions Editor

Art, Design, and Photo

BOOK DESIGN

Richard Metzger, Design Director

Marc Cooper, Senior Designer

Ron Bowdoin, Designer

Alicia Sullivan, Designer (ATE), **Cristina Bowerman,** Design Associate (ATE)

Eric Rupprath, Designer (Ancillaries)

Holly Whittaker, Traffic Coordinator

IMAGE ACQUISITIONS

Joe London, Director

Elaine Tate, Art Buyer Supervisor

Tim Taylor, Photo Research Supervisor

Stephanie Morris, Assistant Photo Researcher

PHOTO STUDIO

Sam Dudgeon, Senior Staff Photographer

Victoria Smith, Photo Specialist

Lauren Eischen, Photo Coordinator

DESIGN NEW MEDIA

Susan Michael, Design Director

Production

Mimi Stockdell, Senior Production Manager

Beth Sample, Senior Production Coordinator

Suzanne Brooks, Sara Carroll-Downs

Media Production

Kim A. Scott, Senior Production Manager

Adriana Bardin-Prestwood, Senior Production Coordinator

New Media

Armin Gutzmer, Director

Jim Bruno, Senior Project Manager

Lydia Doty, Senior Project Manager

Jessica Bega, Project Manager

Cathy Kuhles, Nina Degollado, Technical Assistants

Design Implementation and Production

The Quarasan Group, Inc.

Acknowledgments

Chapter Writers

Christie Borgford, Ph.D.
Professor of Chemistry
University of Alabama
Birmingham, Alabama

Andrew Champagne
Former Physics Teacher
Ashland High School
Ashland, Massachusetts

Mapi Cuevas, Ph.D.
Professor of Chemistry
Santa Fe Community College
Gainesville, Florida

Leila Dumas
Former Physics Teacher
LBJ Science Academy
Austin, Texas

William G. Lamb, Ph.D.
Science Teacher and Dept. Chair
Oregon Episcopal School
Portland, Oregon

Sally Ann Vonderbrink, Ph.D.
Chemistry Teacher
St. Xavier High School
Cincinnati, Ohio

Lab Writers

Phillip G. Bunce
Former Physics Teacher
Bowie High School
Austin, Texas

Kenneth E. Creese
Science Teacher
White Mountain Junior High School
Rock Springs, Wyoming

William G. Lamb, Ph.D.
Science Teacher and Dept. Chair
Oregon Episcopal School
Portland, Oregon

Alyson Mike
Science Teacher
East Valley Middle School
East Helena, Montana

Joseph W. Price
Science Teacher and Dept. Chair
H. M. Browne Junior High School
Washington, D.C.

Denice Lee Sandefur
Science Teacher and Dept. Chair
Nucla High School
Nucla, Colorado

John Spadafino
Mathematics and Physics Teacher
Hackensack High School
Hackensack, New Jersey

Walter Woolbaugh
Science Teacher
Manhattan Junior High School
Manhattan, Montana

Academic Reviewers

Paul R. Berman, Ph.D.
Professor of Physics
University of Michigan
Ann Arbor, Michigan

Russell M. Brengelman, Ph.D.
Professor of Physics
Morehead State University
Morehead, Kentucky

John A. Brockhaus, Ph.D.
Director, Mapping, Charting and Geodesy Program
Department of Geography and Environmental Engineering
United States Military Academy
West Point, New York

Walter Bron, Ph.D.
Professor of Physics
University of California
Irvine, California

Andrew J. Davis, Ph.D.
Manager, ACE Science Center
Department of Physics
California Institute of Technology
Pasadena, California

Peter E. Demmin, Ed.D.
Former Science Teacher and Department Chair
Amherst Central High School
Amherst, New York

Roger Falcone, Ph.D.
Professor of Physics and Department Chair
University of California
Berkeley, California

Cassandra A. Fraser, Ph.D.
Assistant Professor of Chemistry
University of Virginia
Charlottesville, Virginia

L. John Gagliardi, Ph.D.
Associate Professor of Physics and Department Chair
Rutgers University
Camden, New Jersey

Gabriele F. Giuliani, Ph.D.
Professor of Physics
Purdue University
West Lafayette, Indiana

Roy W. Hann, Jr., Ph.D.
Professor of Civil Engineering
Texas A&M University
College Station, Texas

John L. Hubisz, Ph.D.
Professor of Physics
North Carolina State University
Raleigh, North Carolina

Samuel P. Kounaves, Ph.D.
Professor of Chemistry
Tufts University
Medford, Massachusetts

Karol Lang, Ph.D.
Associate Professor of Physics
The University of Texas
Austin, Texas

Gloria Langer, Ph.D.
Professor of Physics
University of Colorado
Boulder, Colorado

Phillip LaRoe
Professor
Helena College of Technology
Helena, Montana

Joseph A. McClure, Ph.D.
Associate Professor of Physics
Georgetown University
Washington, D.C.

LaMoine L. Motz, Ph.D.
Coordinator of Science Education
Department of Learning Services
Oakland County Schools
Waterford, Michigan

R. Thomas Myers, Ph.D.
Professor of Chemistry, Emeritus
Kent State University
Kent, Ohio

Hillary Clement Olson, Ph.D.
Research Associate
Institute for Geophysics
The University of Texas
Austin, Texas

David P. Richardson, Ph.D.
Professor of Chemistry
Thompson Chemical Laboratory
Williams College
Williamstown, Massachusetts

John Rigden, Ph.D.
Director of Special Projects
American Institute of Physics
Colchester, Vermont

Peter Sheridan, Ph.D.
Professor of Chemistry
Colgate University
Hamilton, New York

Vederaman Sriraman, Ph.D.
Associate Professor of Technology
Southwest Texas State University
San Marcos, Texas

Jack B. Swift, Ph.D.
Professor of Physics
The University of Texas
Austin, Texas

Atiq Syed, Ph.D.
Master Instructor of Mathematics and Science
Texas State Technical College
Harlingen, Texas

Leonard Taylor, Ph.D.
Professor Emeritus
Department of Electrical Engineering
University of Maryland
College Park, Maryland

Virginia L. Trimble, Ph.D.
Professor of Physics and Astronomy
University of California
Irvine, California

Acknowledgments (cont.)

Martin VanDyke, Ph.D.
Professor of Chemistry, Emeritus
Front Range Community
    College
Westminster, Colorado

Gabriela Waschewsky, Ph.D.
Science and Math Teacher
Emery High School
Emeryville, California

Safety Reviewer

Jack A. Gerlovich, Ph.D.
Associate Professor
School of Education
Drake University
Des Moines, Iowa

Teacher Reviewers

Barry L. Bishop
Science Teacher and Dept. Chair
San Rafael Junior High School
Ferron, Utah

Paul Boyle
Science Teacher
Perry Heights Middle School
Evansville, Indiana

Kenneth Creese
Science Teacher
White Mountain Junior High
    School
Rock Springs, Wyoming

Vicky Farland
Science Teacher and Dept. Chair
Centennial Middle School
Yuma, Arizona

Rebecca Ferguson
Science Teacher
North Ridge Middle School
North Richland Hills, Texas

Laura Fleet
Science Teacher
Alice B. Landrum Middle
    School
Ponte Vedra Beach, Florida

Jennifer Ford
Science Teacher and Dept. Chair
North Ridge Middle School
North Richland Hills, Texas

Susan Gorman
Science Teacher
North Ridge Middle School
North Richland Hills, Texas

C. John Graves
Science Teacher
Monforton Middle School
Bozeman, Montana

Dennis Hanson
Science Teacher and Dept. Chair
Big Bear Middle School
Big Bear Lake, California

David A. Harris
Science Teacher and Dept. Chair
The Thacher School
Ojai, California

Norman E. Holcomb
Science Teacher
Marion Local Schools
Maria Stein, Ohio

Kenneth J. Horn
Science Teacher and Dept. Chair
Fallston Middle School
Fallston, Maryland

Tracy Jahn
Science Teacher
Berkshire Junior-Senior High
    School
Canaan, New York

Kerry A. Johnson
Science Teacher
Isbell Middle School
Santa Paula, California

Drew E. Kirian
Science Teacher
Solon Middle School
Solon, Ohio

Harriet Knops
Science Teacher and Dept. Chair
Rolling Hills Middle School
El Dorado, California

Scott Mandel, Ph.D.
*Director and Educational
    Consultant*
Teachers Helping Teachers
Los Angeles, California

Thomas Manerchia
Former Science Teacher
Archmere Academy
Claymont, Delaware

Edith McAlanis
Science Teacher and Dept. Chair
Socorro Middle School
El Paso, Texas

Kevin McCurdy, Ph.D.
Science Teacher
Elmwood Junior High School
Rogers, Arkansas

Alyson Mike
Science Teacher
East Valley Middle School
East Helena, Montana

Donna Norwood
Science Teacher and Dept. Chair
Monroe Middle School
Charlotte, North Carolina

Joseph W. Price
Science Teacher and Dept. Chair
H. M. Browne Junior High
    School
Washington, D.C.

Terry J. Rakes
Science Teacher
Elmwood Junior High School
Rogers, Arkansas

Beth Richards
Science Teacher
North Middle School
Crystal Lake, Illinois

Elizabeth J. Rustad
Science Teacher
Crane Middle School
Yuma, Arizona

Rodney A. Sandefur
Science Teacher
Naturita Middle School
Naturita, Colorado

Helen Schiller
Science Teacher
Northwood Middle School
Taylors, South Carolina

Bert J. Sherwood
Science Teacher
Socorro Middle School
El Paso, Texas

Patricia McFarlane Soto
Science Teacher and Dept. Chair
G. W. Carver Middle School
Miami, Florida

David M. Sparks
Science Teacher
Redwater Junior High School
Redwater, Texas

Larry Tackett
Science Teacher and Dept. Chair
Andrew Jackson Middle School
Cross Lanes, West Virginia

Elsie N. Waynes
Science Teacher and Dept. Chair
R. H. Terrell Junior High School
Washington, D.C.

Sharon L. Woolf
Science Teacher
Langston Hughes Middle
    School
Reston, Virginia

Alexis S. Wright
*Middle School Science
    Coordinator*
Rye Country Day School
Rye, New York

Lee Yassinski
Science Teacher
Sun Valley Middle School
Sun Valley, California

John Zambo
Science Teacher
Elizabeth Ustach Middle School
Modesto, California

Sound and Light

Skills Development

Process Skills

QuickLabs

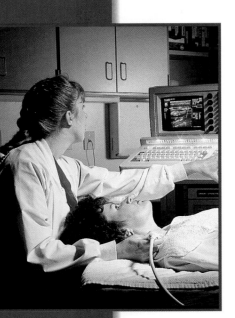

Chapter Labs

Research and Critical Thinking Skills

Apply

Feature Articles

Science, Technology, and Society

Across the Sciences

Science Fiction

Eureka!

Eye on the Environment

Connections

Astronomy Connection

Biology Connection

Environment Connection

Geology Connection

Mathematics

To the Student

This book was created to make your science experience interesting, exciting, and fun!

Go for It!

Science is a process of discovery, a trek into the unknown. The skills you develop using *Holt Science & Technology*—such as observing, experimenting, and explaining observations and ideas—are the skills you will need for the future. There is a universe of exploration and discovery awaiting those who accept the challenges of science.

Science & Technology

You see the interaction between science and technology every day. Science makes technology possible. On the other hand, some of the products of technology, such as computers, are used to make further scientific discoveries. In fact, much of the scientific work that is done today has become so technically complicated and expensive that no one person can do it entirely alone. But make no mistake, the creative ideas for even the most highly technical and expensive scientific work still come from individuals.

Activities and Labs

The activities and labs in this book will allow you to make some basic but important scientific discoveries on your own. You can even do some exploring on your own at home! Here's your chance to use your imagination and curiosity as you investigate your world.

Keep a ScienceLog

In this book, you will be asked to keep a type of journal called a ScienceLog to record your thoughts, observations, experiments, and conclusions. As you develop your ScienceLog, you will see your own ideas taking shape over time. You'll have a written record of how your ideas have changed as you learn about and explore interesting topics in science.

Know "What You'll Do"

The "What You'll Do" list at the beginning of each section is your built-in guide to what you need to learn in each chapter. When you can answer the questions in the Section Review and Chapter Review, you know you are ready for a test.

Check Out the Internet

You will see this logo throughout the book. You'll be using *sci*LINKS as your gateway to the Internet. Once you log on to *sci*LINKS using your computer's Internet link, type in the *sci*LINKS address. When asked for the keyword code, type in the keyword for that topic. A wealth of resources is now at your disposal to help you learn more about that topic.

In addition to *sci*LINKS you can log on to some other great resources to go with your text. The addresses shown below will take you to the home page of each site.

internet connect

This textbook contains the following on-line resources to help you make the most of your science experience.

Visit **go.hrw.com** for extra help and study aids matched to your textbook. Just type in the keyword HST HOME.

Visit **www.scilinks.org** to find resources specific to topics in your textbook. Keywords appear throughout your book to take you further.

 **Smithsonian Institution®**
Internet Connections

Visit **www.si.edu/hrw** for specifically chosen on-line materials from one of our nation's premier science museums.

Visit **www.cnnfyi.com** for late-breaking news and current events stories selected just for you.

The Energy of Waves

Pre-Reading Questions

1. What is a wave?
2. What properties do all waves have?
3. What can happen when waves interact?

CATCH THE WAVE!

A surfer takes advantage of a wave's energy to catch an exciting ride. The ocean wave that this surfer is riding is just one type of wave that you may encounter. You probably are very familiar with water waves, but did you know that waves are also responsible for light, sound, and even earthquakes? From music to television, waves play an important role in your life every day. In this chapter, you will learn about the properties of waves and how waves interact with each other and everything around them.

ENERGETIC WAVES

In this activity, you will observe the movement of a wave. Then you will determine the source of the wave's energy.

Procedure

1. Tie one end of a **piece of rope** to the back of a **chair.**

2. Hold the other end in one hand, and stand away from the chair so that the rope is almost straight but is not pulled tight.

3. Move the rope up and down quickly to create a single wave. Repeat this step several times. Record your observations in your ScienceLog.

Analysis

4. Which direction does the wave move?

5. How does the movement of the rope compare with the movement of the wave?

6. Where does the energy of the wave come from? Make an inference using direct evidence.

TRY at HOME

Terms to Learn

wave   transverse wave
medium   longitudinal wave

What You'll Do

◆ Describe how waves transfer energy without transferring matter.
◆ Distinguish between waves that require a medium and waves that do not.
◆ Explain the difference between transverse and longitudinal waves.

The Nature of Waves

Imagine that your family has just returned home from a day at the beach. You had fun, but you are hungry from playing in the ocean under a hot sun. You put some leftover pizza in the microwave for dinner, and you turn on the radio. Just then, the phone rings. It's your best friend calling to find out if you've done your math homework yet.

In the events described above, how many different waves were present? Believe it or not, at least five can be identified! Can you name them? Here's a hint: A **wave** is any disturbance that transmits energy through matter or space. Okay, here are the answers: water waves in the ocean; microwaves inside the microwave oven; light waves from the sun; radio waves transmitted to the radio; and sound waves from the radio, telephone, and voices. Don't worry if you didn't get very many. You will be able to name them all after you read this section.

Waves Carry Energy

Energy can be carried away from its source by a wave. However, the material through which the wave travels does not move with the energy. For example, sound waves often travel through air, but the air does not travel with the sound. If air were to travel with sound, you would feel a rush of air every time you heard the phone ring! **Figure 1** illustrates how waves carry energy but not matter.

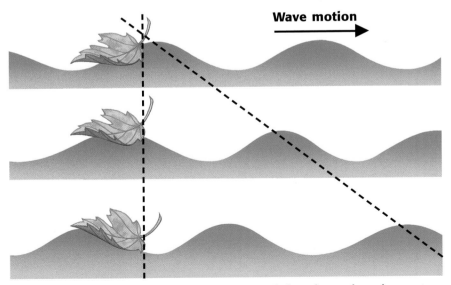

Figure 1 *Waves on a pond move toward the shore, but the water and the leaf floating on the surface do not move with the wave.*

As a wave travels, it uses its energy to do work on every-thing in its path. For example, the waves in a pond do work on the water to make it move up and down. The waves also do work on anything floating on the water's surface—for example, boats and ducks bob up and down with waves.

Energy Transfer Through a Medium Some waves transfer energy by the vibration of particles in a medium. A **medium** is a substance through which a wave can travel. A medium can be a solid, a liquid, or a gas. The plural of *medium* is *media*.

When a particle vibrates (moves back and forth, as in **Figure 2**), it can pass its energy to a particle next to it. As a result, the second particle will vibrate in a way similar to the first particle. In this way, energy is transmitted through a medium.

Sound waves require a medium. Sound energy travels by the vibration of particles in liquids, solids, and gases. If there are no particles to vibrate, no sound is possible. For example, if you put an alarm clock inside a jar and remove all the air from the jar to create a vacuum, you will not be able to hear the alarm.

Other waves that require a medium include ocean waves, which travel through water, and waves on guitar and cello strings. Waves that require a medium are called *mechanical waves*. **Figure 3** shows the effect of another mechanical wave.

Figure 2 *A vibration is one complete back-and-forth motion of an object.*

Figure 3 *Seismic waves travel through the ground. The 1964 earthquake in Alaska changed the features of this area.*

You can see distant objects in space using electromagnetic waves. Turn to page 26 to learn how.

Energy Transfer Without a Medium Some waves can transfer energy without traveling through a medium. Visible light is an example of a wave that doesn't require a medium. Other examples include microwaves produced by microwave ovens, TV and radio signals, and X rays used by dentists and doctors. Waves that do not require a medium are called *electromagnetic waves.*

Although electromagnetic waves do not require a medium, they can travel through substances such as air, water, and glass. However, they travel fastest through empty space. Light from the sun is a type of electromagnetic wave. **Figure 4** shows that light waves from the sun can travel through both space and matter to support life on Earth.

Astronomy

C O N N E C T I O N

Light waves from some stars and galaxies travel distances so great that they can be expressed only in light-years. A light-year is the distance that light travels in a year. Some of the light waves from these stars have traveled billions of light-years before reaching Earth. This means that the light that we see today from some distant stars left the star's surface before the Earth was formed.

Figure 4 *Light waves from the sun travel more than 100 million kilometers through nearly empty space, then more than 300 km through the atmosphere, and then another 10 m through water to support life in and around a coral reef.*

✓ Self-Check

How do mechanical waves differ from electromagnetic waves? *(See page 152 to check your answer.)*

Types of Waves

Waves can be classified based on the direction in which the particles of the medium vibrate compared with the direction in which the waves travel. The two main types of waves are transverse waves and longitudinal (LAHN juh TOOD nuhl) waves. In certain conditions, a transverse wave and a longitudinal wave can combine to form another type of wave, called a surface wave.

Transverse Waves Waves in which the particles vibrate with an up-and-down motion are called **transverse waves.** *Transverse* means "moving across." The particles in a transverse wave move across, or perpendicular to, the direction that the wave is traveling. To be *perpendicular* means to be "at right angles." Try the MathBreak to practice identifying perpendicular lines.

A wave moving on a rope is an example of a transverse wave. In **Figure 5,** you can see that the points along the rope vibrate perpendicular to the direction the wave is traveling. The highest point of a transverse wave is called a *crest,* and the lowest point between each crest is called a *trough.* Although electromagnetic waves do not travel by vibrating particles in a medium, all electromagnetic waves are classified as transverse waves.

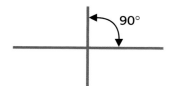
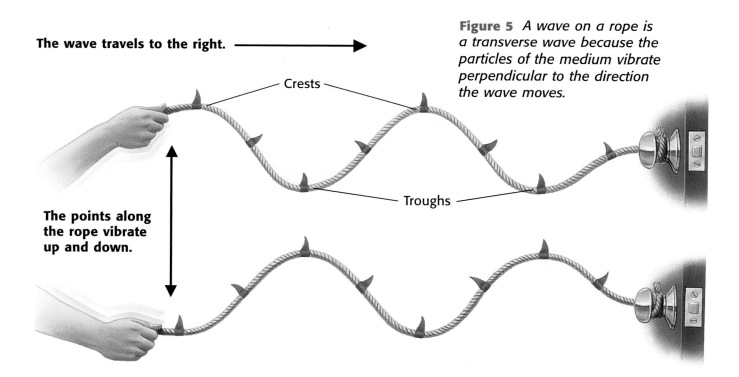

The wave travels to the right. ⟶

The points along the rope vibrate up and down.

Crests

Troughs

Figure 5 *A wave on a rope is a transverse wave because the particles of the medium vibrate perpendicular to the direction the wave moves.*

Longitudinal Waves In a **longitudinal wave,** the particles of the medium vibrate back and forth along the path that the wave travels. You can create a longitudinal wave on a spring, as shown in **Figure 6.**

When you push on the end of the spring, the coils of the spring are crowded together. A section of a longitudinal wave where the particles are crowded together is called a *compression.* When you pull back on the end of the spring, the coils are less crowded than normal. A section where the particles are less crowded than normal is called a *rarefaction* (RER uh FAK shuhn).

Compressions and rarefactions travel along a longitudinal wave much in the way the crests and troughs of a transverse wave move from one end to the other, as shown in **Figure 7.**

Figure 6 *Pushing a spring back and forth creates a longitudinal wave.*

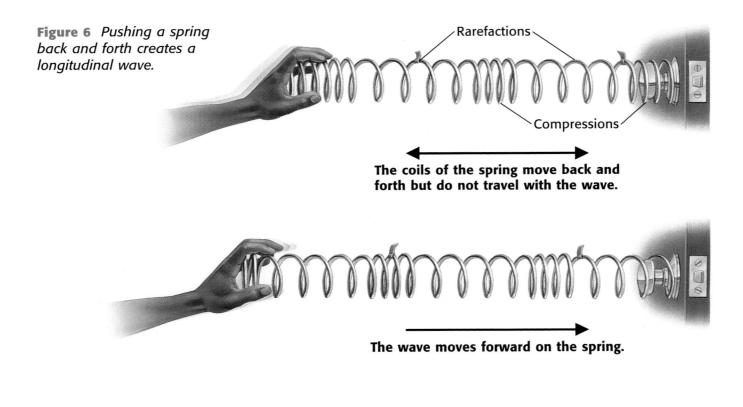

Rarefactions

Compressions

The coils of the spring move back and forth but do not travel with the wave.

The wave moves forward on the spring.

Figure 7 *The compressions of a longitudinal wave are like the crests of a transverse wave, and the rarefactions are like troughs.*

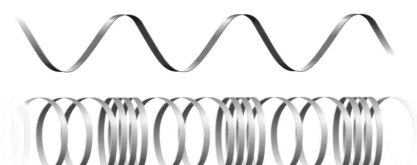

A sound wave is an example of a longitudinal wave. Sound waves travel by compressions and rarefactions of air particles. **Figure 8** shows how a vibrating drumhead creates these compressions and rarefactions.

When the drumhead moves out after being hit, a compression is created in the air particles.

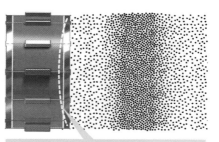

When the drumhead moves back in, a rarefaction is created.

Figure 8 *Sound energy is carried away from a drum in a longitudinal wave.*

Combinations of Waves When waves occur at or near the boundary between two media, a transverse wave and a longitudinal wave can combine to form a *surface wave*. An example is shown in **Figure 9.** Surface waves look like transverse waves, but the particles of the medium in a surface wave move in circles rather than up and down. The particles move forward at the crest of each wave and move backward at the trough. The arrows in Figure 9 show the movement of particles in a surface wave.

Figure 9 *Ocean waves are surface waves because they travel at the water's surface, where the water meets the air. A floating bottle shows the motion of particles in a surface wave.*

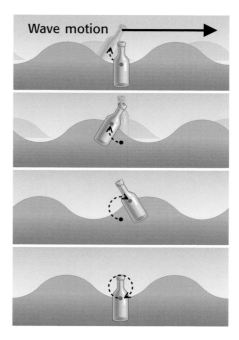

Wave motion

SECTION REVIEW

1. Describe how transverse waves differ from longitudinal waves.

2. Why can't you cause a floating leaf to move to the edge of a pond by throwing stones behind it?

3. Explain why supernova explosions in space can be seen but not heard on Earth.

4. **Applying Concepts** Sometimes people at a sports event do "the wave." Do you think this is a real example of a wave? Why or why not?

internet**connect**

SC*L*INKS.

NSTA

TOPIC: The Nature of Waves, Types of Waves
GO TO: www.scilinks.org
*sci***LINKS NUMBER:** HSTP480, HSTP490

What You'll Do

◆ Identify and describe four wave properties.

◆ Explain how amplitude and frequency are related to the energy of a wave.

Properties of Waves

Imagine that you are canoeing on a lake. You decide to stop paddling for a while and relax in the sunshine. The breeze makes small waves on the water. These waves are short and close together, and they have little effect on the canoe. Then a speedboat roars past you. The speedboat creates tall, widely spaced waves that cause your canoe to rock wildly. So much for relaxation!

Waves have properties that are useful for description and comparison. In this example, you could compare properties such as the height of the waves and the distance between the waves. In this section, you will learn about the properties of waves and how to measure them.

Amplitude

If you tie one end of a rope to the back of a chair, you can create waves by moving the other end up and down. If you move the rope a small distance, you will make a short wave. If you move the rope a greater distance, you will make a tall wave.

The property of waves that is related to the height of a wave is known as amplitude. The **amplitude** of a wave is the maximum distance the wave vibrates from its rest position. The rest position is where the particles of a medium stay when there are no disturbances. The larger the amplitude is, the taller the wave is. **Figure 10** shows how the amplitude of a transverse wave is measured.

Figure 10 *The amplitude of a transverse wave is measured from the rest position to the crest or to the trough of the wave.*

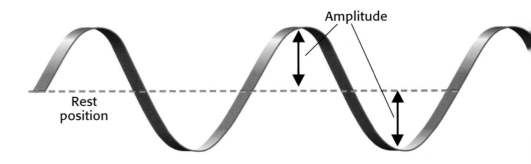

Larger Amplitude Means More Energy   When using a rope to make waves, you have to work harder to create a wave with a large amplitude than to create one with a small amplitude. This is because it takes more energy to move the rope farther from its rest position. Therefore, a wave with a large amplitude carries more energy than a wave with a small amplitude, as shown in **Figure 11.**

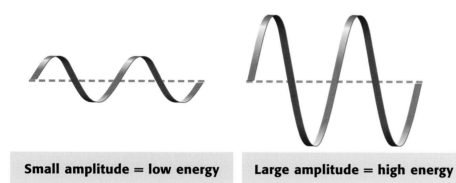

Small amplitude = low energy   **Large amplitude = high energy**

Figure 11 *The amplitude of a wave depends on the amount of energy.*

Wavelength

Another property of waves is wavelength. A **wavelength** is the distance between any two adjacent crests or compressions in a series of waves. The distance between two adjacent troughs or rarefactions is also a wavelength. In fact, the wavelength can be measured from any point on one wave to the corresponding point on the next wave. All of the measurements will be equal, as shown in **Figure 12.**

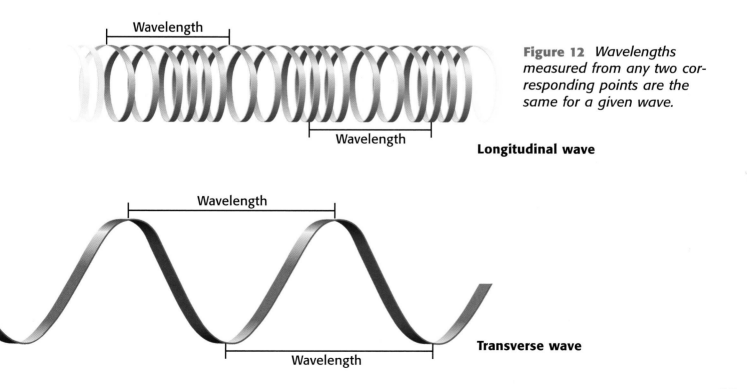

Figure 12 *Wavelengths measured from any two corresponding points are the same for a given wave.*

Wavelength

Wavelength

Longitudinal wave

Wavelength

Wavelength

Transverse wave

Frequency

Think about making rope waves again. The number of waves that you can make in 1 second depends on how quickly you move the rope. If you move the rope slowly, you make only a small number of waves each second. If you move it quickly, you make a large number of waves. The number of waves produced in a given amount of time is the **frequency** of the wave.

Measuring Frequency   You can measure frequency by counting either the number of crests or the number of troughs that pass a point in a certain amount of time. If you were measuring the frequency of a longitudinal wave, you would count the number of compressions or rarefactions. Frequency is usually expressed in *hertz* (Hz). For waves, one hertz equals one wave per second (1 Hz = 1/s). The frequency of a wave is related to its wavelength, as shown in **Figure 13.**

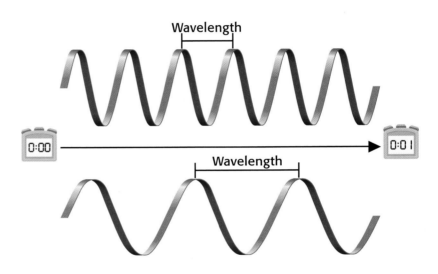

Figure 13 *At a given speed, the higher the frequency is, the shorter the wavelength.*

Spring into action! Find the speed of waves on a spring toy. Turn to page 126 of the LabBook.

Higher Frequency Means More Energy   It takes more energy to vibrate a rope quickly than to vibrate a rope slowly. If the amplitudes are equal, high-frequency waves carry more energy than low-frequency waves. In Figure 13, the top wave carries more energy than the bottom wave.

Because frequency and wavelength are so closely related, you can also relate the amount of energy carried by a wave to the wavelength. In general, a wave with a short wavelength carries more energy than a wave with a long wavelength.

Wave Speed

Another property of waves is **wave speed**—the speed at which a wave travels. Speed is the distance traveled over time, so wave speed can be found by measuring the distance a single crest or compression travels in a given amount of time.

The speed of a wave depends on the medium in which the wave is traveling. For example, the wave speed of sound in air is about 340 m/s, but the wave speed of sound in steel is about 5,200 m/s.

Calculating Wave Speed   Wave speed can be calculated using wavelength and frequency. The relationship between wave speed (v), wavelength (λ, the Greek letter lambda), and frequency (f) is expressed in the following equation:

$$v = \lambda \times f$$

You can see in **Figure 14** how this equation can be used to determine wave speed. Try the MathBreak to practice using this equation.

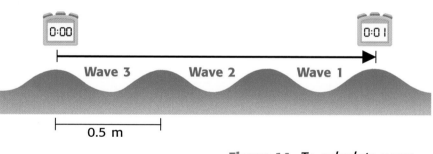

λ = 0.5 m   f = 3 Hz (3/s)
v = 0.5 m × 3 Hz = 1.5 m/s

Figure 14 *To calculate wave speed, multiply the wavelength by the number of waves that pass in 1 second (frequency).*

MATH BREAK

Wave Calculations

The equation for wave speed can be rearranged to determine wavelength (λ) or frequency (f).

$$\lambda = \frac{v}{f} \qquad f = \frac{v}{\lambda}$$

You can determine the wavelength of a wave with a speed of 20 m/s and a frequency of 4 Hz like this:

$$\lambda = \frac{v}{f}$$

$$\lambda = 20 \text{ m/s} \div 4 \text{ Hz}$$

$$\lambda = \frac{20 \text{ m}}{\cancel{s}} \times \frac{1\cancel{s}}{4}$$

$$\lambda = 5 \text{ m}$$

Now It's Your Turn

1. What is the frequency of a wave if it has a speed of 12 cm/s and a wavelength of 3 cm?

2. A wave has a frequency of 5 Hz and a wave speed of 18 m/s. What is its wavelength?

SECTION REVIEW

1. Draw a transverse wave, and identify its amplitude and wavelength.

2. What is the speed (v) of a wave that has a wavelength (λ) of 2 m and a frequency (f) of 6 Hz?

3. **Inferring Conclusions**   Compare the amplitudes and frequencies of the two types of waves discussed at the beginning of this section, and infer which type of wave carried the most energy. Explain your answer.

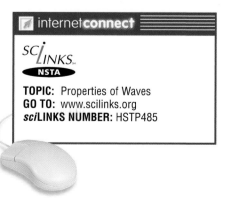

internet**connect**

SC*LINKS*

NSTA

TOPIC: Properties of Waves
GO TO: www.scilinks.org
*sci*LINKS NUMBER: HSTP485

Terms to Learn

reflection   interference
refraction   standing wave
diffraction   resonance

What You'll Do

◆ Describe reflection, refraction, diffraction, and interference.
◆ Compare destructive interference with constructive interference.
◆ Describe resonance, and give examples.

Wave Interactions

Imagine that you wake up early one morning before the sun has risen and go outside. You look up and notice that a full moon is high in the sky, and the stars are twinkling brilliantly, as shown in **Figure 15.** The sky is so clear you can find constellations (groupings of stars), such as the Big Dipper and Cassiopeia, and planets, such as Venus and Mars.

All stars, including the sun, produce light. But planets and the moon do not produce light. So why do they shine so brightly? Light from the sun *reflects* off the planets and the moon. Reflection is one of the wave interactions that you will learn about in this section.

Figure 15 *A wave interaction is responsible for this beautiful morning scene.*

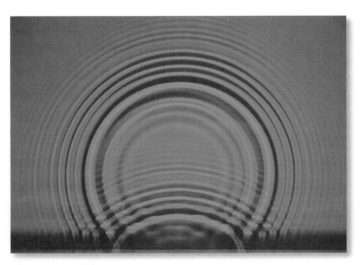

Figure 16 *These water waves are reflecting off the side of the container.*

Reflection

Reflection occurs when a wave bounces back after striking a barrier. All waves—including water, sound, and light waves—can be reflected. The reflection of water waves is shown in **Figure 16.** Reflected sound waves are called *echoes,* and light waves reflecting off an object allow you to see that object. For example, light waves from the sun are reflected when they strike the surface of the moon. These reflected waves allow us to enjoy moonlit nights.

Refraction

Try this simple experiment: place a pencil in a half-filled glass of water. Now look at the pencil from the side. The pencil appears to be broken into two pieces! But when you take the pencil out of the water, it is perfectly fine.

What you observed in this experiment was the result of the refraction of light waves. **Refraction** is the bending of a wave as it passes at an angle from one medium to another.

Remember that the speed of a wave varies depending on the medium in which the wave is traveling. So when a wave moves from one medium to another, the wave's speed changes. When a wave enters a new medium at an angle, the part of the wave that enters first begins traveling at a different speed from the rest of the wave. This causes the wave to bend, as shown in **Figure 17.**

Wave crests

Figure 17 *Light waves passing at an angle into a new medium—such as water—are refracted because the speed of the waves changes.*

✓ Self-Check

Will a light wave refract if it enters a new medium perpendicular to the surface? Explain. *(See page 152 to check your answer.)*

Diffraction

Suppose you are walking down a city street and you hear music. The sound seems to be coming from around the corner, but you cannot see who is playing the music because the building on the corner blocks your view. Why is it that sound waves travel around a corner better than light waves do?

Most of the time, waves travel in straight lines. For example, a beam of light from a flashlight is fairly straight. But in some circumstances, waves curve or bend when they reach the edge of an object. The bending of waves around a barrier or through an opening is known as **diffraction.**

Activity

Light waves diffract around corners of buildings much less than sound waves. Imagine what would happen if light waves diffracted around corners much more than sound waves. Write a paragraph describing how this would change what you see and hear as you walk around your neighborhood.

TRY at HOME

Figure 18 Diffraction of Waves

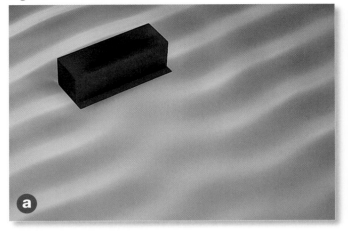

a

When the barrier or opening is the same size as or is smaller than the wavelength of an approaching wave, the amount of diffraction is large.

b

If the barrier or opening is larger than the wavelength of the wave, there is only a small amount of diffraction.

The amount of diffraction a wave experiences depends on its wavelength and the size of the barrier or opening the wave encounters, as shown in **Figure 18.** You can hear music around the corner of a building because sound waves have long wavelengths and are able to diffract around corners. However, you cannot see who is playing the music because the wavelengths of light waves are much smaller than the building, so light is not diffracted very much.

Interference

You know that all matter has volume. Therefore, objects cannot occupy the same space at the same time. But because waves are energy and not matter, more than one wave can exist in the same place at the same time. In fact, two waves can meet, share the same space, and pass through each other! When two or more waves share the same space, they overlap. The result of two or more waves overlapping is called **interference. Figure 19** shows one situation where waves occupy the same space.

Figure 19 *When sound waves from several instruments combine through interference, the result is a wave with a larger amplitude, which means a louder sound.*

Constructive Interference Increases Amplitude *Constructive interference* occurs when the crests of one wave overlap the crests of another wave or waves. The troughs of the waves also overlap. An example of constructive interference is shown in **Figure 20.** When waves combine in this way, the result is a new wave with higher crests and deeper troughs than the original waves. In other words, the resulting wave has a larger amplitude than the original waves had.

Figure 20 *When waves combine by constructive interference, the resulting wave has an amplitude that is larger than those of the original waves. After the waves interfere, they continue traveling in their original directions.*

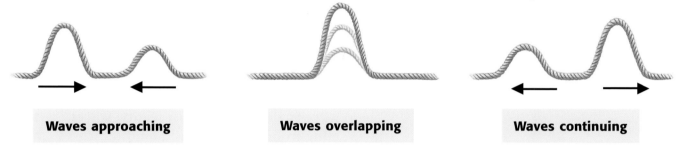

| **Waves approaching** | **Waves overlapping** | **Waves continuing** |

Destructive Interference Decreases Amplitude *Destructive interference* occurs when the crests of one wave and the troughs of another wave overlap. The resulting wave has a smaller amplitude than the original waves had. What do you think happens when the waves involved in destructive interference have the same amplitude? Find out in **Figure 21.**

Figure 21 *When two waves with the same amplitude combine by destructive interference, they cancel each other out. This is called* total destructive interference.

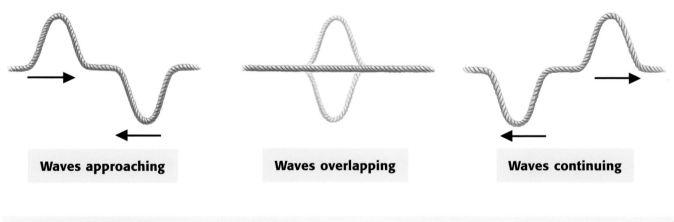

| **Waves approaching** | **Waves overlapping** | **Waves continuing** |

Sound Waves in Movie Theaters

Movie theaters use large screens and several speakers to make your moviegoing experience exciting. Theater designers know that increasing the amplitude of sound waves increases the volume of the sound. In terms of interference, how do you think the positioning of the speakers adds to the excitement?

Speakers

Speakers

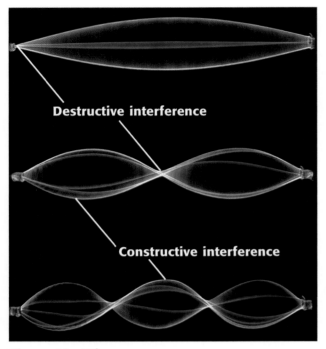

Destructive interference

Constructive interference

Figure 22 *When you move a rope at certain frequencies, you can create different standing waves.*

Interference Can Create Standing Waves

If you tie one end of a rope to the back of a chair and move the other end up and down, the waves you create travel down the rope and are reflected back. If you move the rope at certain frequencies, the rope appears to vibrate in loops, as shown in **Figure 22.** The loops result from the interference between the wave you created and the reflected wave. The resulting wave is called a standing wave. A **standing wave** is a wave that forms a stationary pattern in which portions of the wave are at the rest position due to total destructive interference and other portions have a large amplitude due to constructive interference. However, it only *looks* as if the wave is standing still. In reality, waves are traveling in both directions. Standing waves can be formed with transverse waves, as shown here, as well as with longitudinal waves.

One Object Causes Another to Vibrate During Resonance

As shown above, standing waves can occur at more than one frequency. The frequencies at which standing waves are produced are called *resonant frequencies.* When an object vibrating at or near the resonant frequency of a second object causes the second object to vibrate, **resonance** occurs. A resonating object absorbs energy from the vibrating object and therefore vibrates, too. An example of resonance is shown in **Figure 23.**

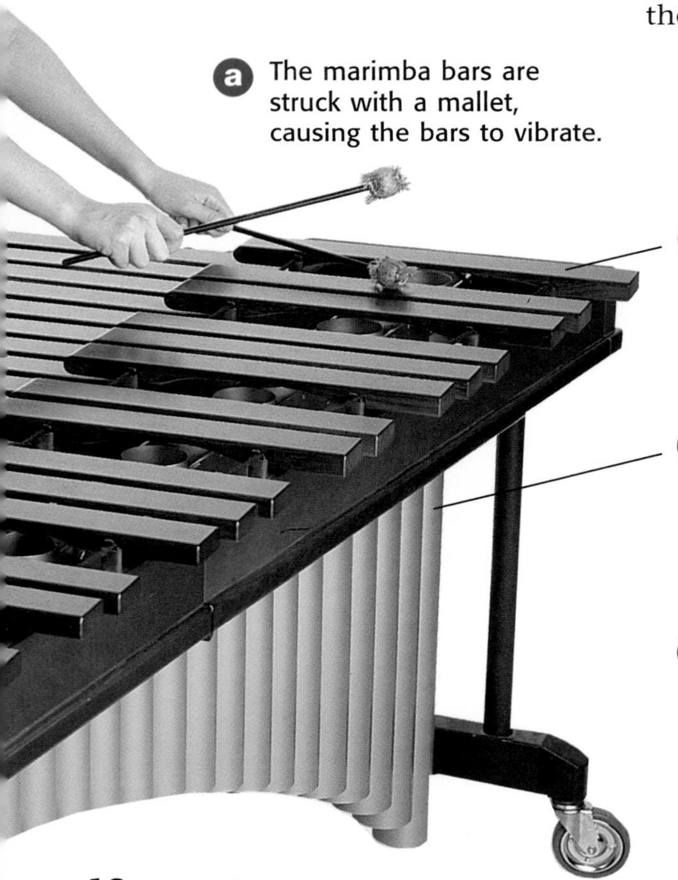

a The marimba bars are struck with a mallet, causing the bars to vibrate.

b The vibrating bars cause the air in the columns to vibrate.

Figure 23 *A marimba produces notes through the resonance of air columns.*

c The lengths of the columns have been adjusted so that the resonant frequency of the air column matches the frequency of the bar.

d The air column resonates with the bar, increasing the amplitude of the vibrations to produce a loud note.

The Tacoma Narrows Bridge Resonance was partially responsible for the destruction of the Tacoma Narrows Bridge, in Washington. The bridge opened in July 1940 and soon earned the nickname Galloping Gertie because of its wavelike motions. These motions were created by wind that blew across the bridge. The wind caused vibrations that were close to a resonant frequency of the bridge. Because the bridge was in resonance, it absorbed a large amount of energy from the wind, which caused it to vibrate with a large amplitude.

On November 7, 1940, a supporting cable slipped, and the bridge began to twist. The twisting of the bridge, combined with high winds, further increased the amplitude of the bridge's motion. Within hours, the amplitude became so great that the bridge collapsed, as shown in **Figure 24.** Luckily, all the people on the bridge that day were able to escape before it crashed into the river below.

Resonance caused the collapse of a bridge near Manchester, England, in 1831. Cavalry troops marched across the bridge in rhythm with its resonant frequency. This caused the bridge to vibrate with a large amplitude and eventually to fall. Since that time, all troops are ordered to "break step" when they cross a bridge.

Figure 24 *The twisting motion that led to the destruction of the bridge was partially caused by resonance.*

SECTION REVIEW

1. Name two wave interactions that can occur when a wave encounters a barrier.

2. Describe what happens when a wave is refracted.

3. **Inferring Relationships** Sometimes when music is played loudly, you can feel your body shake. Explain what is happening in terms of resonance.

internetconnect

SciLINKS
NSTA

TOPIC: Interactions of Waves
GO TO: www.scilinks.org
*sci*LINKS **NUMBER:** HSTP495

Discovery Lab

Wave Energy and Speed

If you threw a small rock into a pond, waves would carry energy away from the point of origin. But if you threw a large rock into a pond, would the waves carry more energy away from the point of origin than waves created by a small rock? Would a large rock create waves that move faster than waves created by a small rock? In this lab, you'll answer these questions.

MATERIALS

🥽 👕

- shallow pan, approximately 20 cm × 30 cm
- newspaper
- plastic cup
- water
- 2 pencils
- stopwatch

Ask a Question

1 Do waves created by a large disturbance carry more energy than waves created by a small disturbance? Do waves created by a large disturbance travel faster than waves created by a small disturbance?

Form a Hypothesis

2 In your ScienceLog, write a few sentences that answer the questions above.

Test the Hypothesis

3 Place the pan on a few sheets of newspaper. Using the plastic cup, fill the pan with water.

4 Make sure that the water is still. Tap the surface of the water near one end of the pan with the eraser end of one pencil. This tap represents the small disturbance. In your ScienceLog, record your observations about the size of the waves that are created and the path that they take.

5 Repeat step 4. This time, use the stopwatch to measure the time it takes for one of the waves to reach the other side of the pan. Record your data in your ScienceLog. Perform this measurement two more times, and take the average of the three trials.

6 Repeat steps 4 and 5 using two pencils at once. The tap with the two pencils represents the large disturbance. (Try tapping the water using the same amount of force that you used with just one pencil.)

Analyze the Results

7 Compare the appearance of the waves created by one pencil with the appearance of the waves created by two pencils. Were there any differences in amplitude (wave height)?

8 Compare the amount of time required for the waves to reach the side of the pan. Did the waves travel faster when you used two pencils?

Draw Conclusions

9 Do waves created by a large disturbance carry more energy than waves created by a small disturbance? Communicate a valid conclusion, using your results. (Hint: Remember the relationship between amplitude and energy.)

10 Do waves created by a large disturbance travel faster than waves created by a small disturbance? Explain your answer.

Going Further

A tsunami is a giant ocean wave that can reach a height of 30 m. Tsunamis that reach land can cause injury and enormous property damage. Using what you just learned about wave energy and speed, explain why tsunamis are so dangerous. Make an inference about how scientists can predict when tsunamis will reach land.

Chapter Highlights

Vocabulary

wave *(p. 4)*
medium *(p. 5)*
transverse wave *(p. 7)*
longitudinal wave *(p. 8)*

Section Notes

• A wave is a disturbance that transmits energy.

• A medium is a substance through which a wave can travel. The particles of a medium do not travel with the wave.

• Waves that require a medium are called mechanical waves. Waves that do not require a medium are called electromagnetic waves.

• Particles in a transverse wave vibrate perpendicular to the direction the wave travels.

• Particles in a longitudinal wave vibrate back and forth in the same direction that the wave travels.

• Transverse and longitudinal waves can combine to form surface waves.

Vocabulary

amplitude *(p. 10)*
wavelength *(p. 11)*
frequency *(p. 12)*
wave speed *(p. 13)*

Section Notes

• Amplitude is the maximum distance the particles in a wave vibrate from their rest position. Large-amplitude waves carry more energy than small-amplitude waves.

• Wavelength is the distance between two adjacent crests (or compressions) of a wave.

• Frequency is the number of waves that pass a given point in a given amount of time. High-frequency waves carry more energy than low-frequency waves.

☑ Skills Check

Math Concepts

WAVE-SPEED CALCULATIONS   The relationship between wave speed (v), wavelength (λ), and frequency (f) is expressed by the equation:

$$v = \lambda \times f$$

For example, if a wave has a wavelength of 1 m and a frequency of 6 Hz (6/s), the wave speed is calculated as follows:

$$v = 1 \text{ m} \times 6 \text{ Hz} = 1 \text{ m} \times 6/\text{s}$$
$$v = 6 \text{ m/s}$$

Visual Understanding

TRANSVERSE AND LONGITUDINAL WAVES
Two common types of waves are transverse waves (shown below) and longitudinal waves. Study Figure 5 on page 7 and Figure 6 on page 8 to review the differences between these two types of waves.

SECTION 2

- Wave speed is the speed at which a wave travels. Wave speed can be calculated by multiplying the wavelength by the wave's frequency.

Labs

Wave Speed, Frequency, and Wavelength *(p. 126)*

SECTION 3

Vocabulary

reflection *(p. 14)*

refraction *(p. 15)*

diffraction *(p. 15)*

interference *(p. 16)*

standing wave *(p. 18)*

resonance *(p. 18)*

Section Notes

- Waves bounce back after striking a barrier during reflection.

- Refraction is the bending of a wave when it passes at an angle from one medium to another.

- Waves bend around barriers or through openings during diffraction. The amount of diffraction depends on the wavelength of the waves and the size of the barrier or opening.

- The result of two or more waves overlapping is called interference.

- Amplitude increases during constructive interference and decreases during destructive interference.

- Standing waves are waves in which portions of the wave do not move and other portions move with a large amplitude.

- Resonance occurs when a vibrating object causes another object to vibrate at one of its resonant frequencies.

Chapter Review

USING VOCABULARY

For each pair of terms, explain the difference in their meanings.

1. longitudinal wave/transverse wave

2. frequency/wave speed

3. wavelength/amplitude

4. reflection/refraction

5. constructive interference/destructive interference

UNDERSTANDING CONCEPTS

Multiple Choice

6. As the wavelength increases, the frequency
   a. decreases.
   b. increases.
   c. remains the same.
   d. increases, then decreases.

7. Which wave interaction explains why sound waves can be heard around corners?
   a. reflection   c. diffraction
   b. refraction   d. interference

8. Refraction occurs when a wave enters a new medium at an angle because
   a. the frequency changes.
   b. the amplitude changes.
   c. the wave speed changes.
   d. None of the above

9. The speed of a wave with a frequency of 2 Hz (2/s), an amplitude of 3 m, and a wavelength of 10 m is
   a. 0.2 m/s.   c. 12 m/s.
   b. 5 m/s.   d. 20 m/s.

10. Waves transfer
    a. matter.   c. particles.
    b. energy.   d. water.

11. A wave that is a combination of longitudinal and transverse waves is a
    a. sound wave.   c. rope wave.
    b. light wave.   d. surface wave.

12. The wave property that is related to the height of a wave is the
    a. wavelength.   c. frequency.
    b. amplitude.   d. wave speed.

13. During constructive interference,
    a. the amplitude increases.
    b. the frequency decreases.
    c. the wave speed increases.
    d. All of the above

14. Waves that don't require a medium are
    a. longitudinal waves.
    b. electromagnetic waves.
    c. surface waves.
    d. mechanical waves.

Short Answer

15. Draw a transverse and a longitudinal wave. Label a crest, a trough, a compression, a rarefaction, and wavelengths. Also label the amplitude on the transverse wave.

16. What is the relationship between frequency, wave speed, and wavelength?

17. Explain how two waves can cancel each other out.

Concept Mapping

18. Use the following terms to create a concept map: wave, refraction, transverse wave, longitudinal wave, wavelength, wave speed, diffraction.

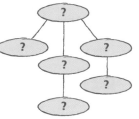

CRITICAL THINKING AND PROBLEM SOLVING

19. After you set up stereo speakers in your school's music room, you notice that in certain areas of the room the sound from the speakers is very loud and in other areas the sound is very soft. Explain how interference causes this.

20. You have lost the paddles for the canoe you rented, and the canoe has drifted to the center of the pond. You need to get the canoe back to shore, but you do not want to get wet by swimming in the pond. Your friend on the shore wants to throw rocks behind the canoe to create waves that will push the canoe toward shore. Will this solution work? Why or why not?

21. Some opera singers have voices so powerful they can break crystal glasses! To do this, they sing one note very loudly and hold it for a long time. The walls of the glass move back and forth until the glass shatters. Explain how this happens in terms of resonance.

MATH IN SCIENCE

22. A fisherman in a rowboat notices that one wave crest passes his fishing line every 5 seconds. He estimates the distance between the crests to be 2 m and estimates the crests of the waves to be 0.4 m above the troughs. Using these data, determine the amplitude and wave speed of the waves. Remember that wave speed is calculated with the formula $v = \lambda \times f$.

INTERPRETING GRAPHICS

23. Rank the waves below from highest energy to lowest energy, and explain your reasoning.

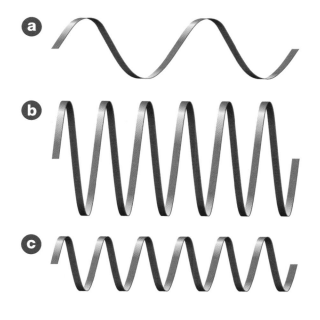

Reading Check-up

Take a minute to review your answers to the Pre-Reading Questions found at the bottom of page 2. Have your answers changed? If necessary, revise your answers based on what you have learned since you began this chapter.

Science, Technology, and Society

The Ultimate Telescope

The largest telescopes in the world don't depend on visible light, lenses, or mirrors. Instead, they collect radio waves from the far reaches of outer space. One radio telescope, called the Very Large Array (VLA), is located in a remote desert in New Mexico.

From Radio Waves to Computer Images

Objects in space give off radio waves that radio telescopes collect. A bowl-shaped dish called a reflector focuses the radio waves onto a small radio antenna hung over the center of the dish. The antenna converts the waves into electric signals. The signals are relayed to a radio receiver, where they are amplified and recorded on tape that can be read by a computer. The computer combines the signals to create an image of the source of the radio waves.

A Marvel at "Seeing"

Radio telescopes have some distinct advantages over optical telescopes. They can "see" objects that are as far as 13 billion light-years away. They can even detect objects that don't release any light at all. Radio telescopes can be used in any kind of weather, can receive signals through atmospheric pollution, and can even penetrate the cosmic dust and gas clouds that occupy vast areas of space. However, radio telescopes must be large in order to be accurate.

Telescope Teamwork

The VLA is an array of 27 separate radio telescopes mounted on railroad tracks and electronically linked by computers. Each of the

▲ *Only a few of the 27 radio telescopes of the VLA, near Datil, New Mexico, can be seen in this photograph.*

27 reflectors is 25 m in diameter. When they operate together, they work like a single telescope with a diameter of 47 km! Using the VLA, astronomers have been able to explore distant galaxies, pulsars, quasars, and possible black holes.

A system of telescopes even larger than the VLA has been used. In the Very Long Baseline Array (VLBA), radio telescopes in different parts of the world all work together. The result is a telescope that is almost as large as the Earth itself!

What Do They See?

▶ Find out about some of the objects "seen" by the VLA, such as pulsars, quasars, and possible black holes. Prepare a report or create a model of one of the objects, and make a presentation to your class. Use diagrams and photographs to make your presentation more interesting.

26

Sounds of Silence

It's morning on the African savanna. Suddenly, without a sound, a family of elephants stops eating and begins to move off. At the same moment, about 6 km away, other members of the same family move off in a direction that will reunite them with the first group. How did the groups know when it was time to go?

Do You Hear What I Hear?

Elephants do much of their communicating by infrasound. This is sound energy with a frequency too low to be heard by humans. These infrasonic conversations take place through deep, soft rumblings produced by the animals. Though humans can't hear the sounds, elephants as far as 10 km away respond quickly to the messages.

Because scientists couldn't hear the elephant "conversations," they couldn't understand how the animals coordinated their activities. Of course, the elephants, which have superb low-frequency hearing, heard the messages clearly. It turns out that much elephant behavior is affected by infrasonic messages. For instance, one kind of rumble from a mother to her calf tells the calf it is all right to nurse. Another rumble, from the group's leader, is the "time to move on" message. Still another infrasonic message may be sent to other elephant groups in the area, warning them of danger.

Radio Collars

Once scientists learned about elephants' infrasonic abilities, they devised ways to study the sounds. Researchers developed radio collars for individual animals to wear. The collars are connected to a computer that helps researchers identify which elephant sent the message. The collars also record the messages. This information helps scientists understand both the messages and the social organization of the group.

Let's Talk

Elephants have developed several ways to "talk" to each other. For example, they greet each other by touching trunks and tusks. And elephants have as many as 25 vocal calls, including the familiar bellowing trumpet call (a sign of great excitement). In other situations, they use chemical signals.

▲ *Two elephants greeting each other*

Recently, researchers recording elephant communications found that when elephants vocalize their low-frequency sounds, they create seismic waves. Elephant messages sent by these underground energy waves may be felt more than 8 km away. Clearly, there is a lot more to elephant conversations than meets the ear!

On Your Own

▶ Elephants are very intelligent and highly sociable. Find out more about the complex social structure of elephant groups. Why is it important for scientists to understand how elephants communicate with each other? How can that understanding help elephants?

The Nature of Sound

Pre-Reading
Questions

1. How does sound travel
   from one place to
   another?

2. What determines a sound's
   pitch and loudness?

3. What can happen when
   sound waves interact with
   each other?

Sound Under the Sea

Look at these dolphins swimming swiftly and silently
through their watery world. Wait a minute—swiftly? Yes.
Silently? No way! Dolphins use sound to communicate.
In fact, each dolphin has a special whistle that it uses to
identify itself. Dolphins also use sound to locate their food
and find their way through murky water. In this chapter,
you'll learn more about the properties and the interactions
of sound waves. You'll also learn how sound is used to
locate objects.

A HOMEMADE GUITAR

In this chapter, you will learn about sound. You can start by making your own guitar. It won't sound as good as a real guitar, but it will help you explore the nature of sound.

Procedure

1. Stretch a **rubber band** lengthwise around an empty **shoe box.** Gently pluck the rubber band. In your ScienceLog, describe what you hear.

2. Stretch **another rubber band of a different thickness** around the box. Pluck both rubber bands. Describe the difference in the sounds.

3. Put a **pencil** across the center of the box and under the rubber bands, and pluck again. Compare this sound with the sound you heard before the pencil was used.

4. Move the pencil closer to one end of the shoe box. Pluck on both sides of the pencil. Describe the differences in the sounds you hear.

Analysis

5. How did the thicknesses of the rubber bands affect the sound?

6. In steps 3 and 4, you changed the length of the rubber bands. What is the relationship between the length of the rubber band and the sound that you hear?

Terms to Learn

wave
medium
outer ear
middle ear
inner ear

What You'll Do

◆ Describe how sound is caused by vibrations.
◆ Explain how sound is transmitted through a medium.
◆ Explain how the human ear works, and identify its parts.

QuickLab

Good Vibrations

1. Gently strike a **tuning fork** on a **rubber eraser.** Watch the prongs, and listen for a sound. Describe what you see and hear.

2. Lightly touch the fork with your fingers. What do you feel?

3. Grasp the prongs of the fork firmly with your hand. What happens to the sound?

4. Strike the tuning fork on the stopper again, and dip the prongs in a **cup of water.** Describe what happens to the water.

5. Record your observations in your ScienceLog.

What Is Sound?

Think about all the sounds you hear every day. Indoors, you might hear people talking, the radio blaring, or dishes clattering in the kitchen sink. Outdoors, you might hear birds singing, cars driving by, or a mosquito buzzing in your ear. That's a lot of different sounds! In this section, you'll explore some common characteristics of the different sounds you hear.

Sound Is Produced by Vibrations

As different as they are, all sounds have some things in common. One characteristic of sound is that it is created by vibrations. A *vibration* is the complete back-and-forth motion of an object. **Figure 1** shows an example of how sound is created by vibrations.

Figure 1 Sounds from a Stereo Speaker

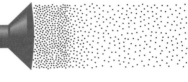

a As the speaker cone moves forward, it pushes the air particles in front of it closer together, creating a region of higher density and pressure called a *compression.*

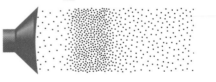

b As the speaker cone moves backward, air particles close to the cone become less crowded, creating a region of lower density and pressure called a *rarefaction.*

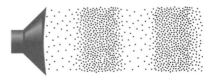

c Every time the cone vibrates, compression and rarefaction are formed. As the compressions and rarefactions travel away from the speaker, sound is transmitted through the air.

Sound Travels as Longitudinal Waves A **wave** is a disturbance that transmits energy through matter or space. In a longitudinal wave, particles vibrate back and forth along the path that the wave travels. Longitudinal (LAHN juh TOOD nuhl) waves consist of compressions and rarefactions. Sound is transmitted through the vibrations and collisions of particles of matter, such as air particles. Because the particles vibrate back and forth along the paths that sound travels, sound travels as longitudinal waves.

Sound waves travel in all directions away from their source as illustrated in **Figure 2.** However, air or other matter does not travel with the sound waves. The particles of air only vibrate back and forth in place. If air did travel with sound, wind gusts from music speakers would blow you over at a school dance!

Biology
C O N N E C T I O N

The vibrations that produce your voice are made inside your throat. When you speak, laugh, or sing, your lungs force air up your windpipe, causing your vocal cords to vibrate.

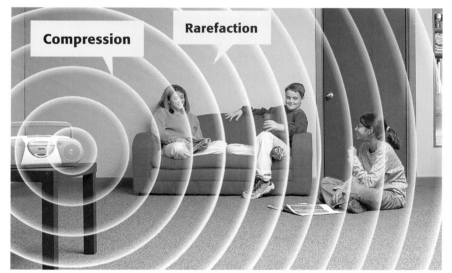

Compression

Rarefaction

Figure 2 *You can't actually see sound waves, but they can be represented by spheres that spread out in all directions.*

Creating Sound Vs. Detecting Sound

Have you heard this riddle before? If a tree falls in the forest and no one is around to hear it, does the tree make a sound?

Think about this situation for a minute. When a tree falls and hits the ground, the tree and the ground vibrate. These vibrations create compressions and rarefactions in the surrounding air. So, yes, there would be a sound!

Making sound is separate from detecting sound. The fact that no one heard the tree fall doesn't mean that there wasn't a sound. A sound was created—it just wasn't detected.

Figure 3 *You can still hear traffic sounds when you are in a car because sound waves can travel through the glass windows and metal body of the car.*

Sound Waves Require a Medium

Another characteristic of sound is that all sound waves require a medium. A **medium** is a substance through which a wave can travel. In the example of a falling tree on the previous page, the medium is air. Most of the sounds that you hear travel through air at least part of the time. But sound waves can also travel through other materials, such as water, glass, and metal, as shown in **Figure 3.**

What would happen if a tree fell in a vacuum? No sound would be created because in a vacuum, there are no air particles to vibrate. Sound cannot travel in a vacuum. This helps to explain the effect described in **Figure 4.** Sound must travel through air or some other medium to reach your ears and be detected.

Figure 4 *Tubing is connected to a pump that is removing air from the jar. As the air is removed, the ringing alarm clock gets quieter and quieter.*

Astronomy

C O N N E C T I O N

The moon has no atmosphere, so there is no air through which sound can travel. The astronauts who walked on the moon had to use radios to talk to each other even when they were standing side by side. Radio waves could travel between the astronauts because they are electromagnetic waves, which don't require a medium. The radio speakers were inside the astronauts' helmets, which were filled with air for the astronauts to breathe.

How You Detect Sound

Imagine you are watching a suspenseful movie. Just before a door is opened, the background music becomes louder. You know that there is something scary behind that door! Now imagine watching the same scene without the sound. It's hard to figure out what's going on without sound to help you understand what you see. Your ears play an important role in this understanding. On the next page, you will see how your ears convert sound waves into electrical signals, which are then sent to your brain for interpretation.

How the Human Ear Works

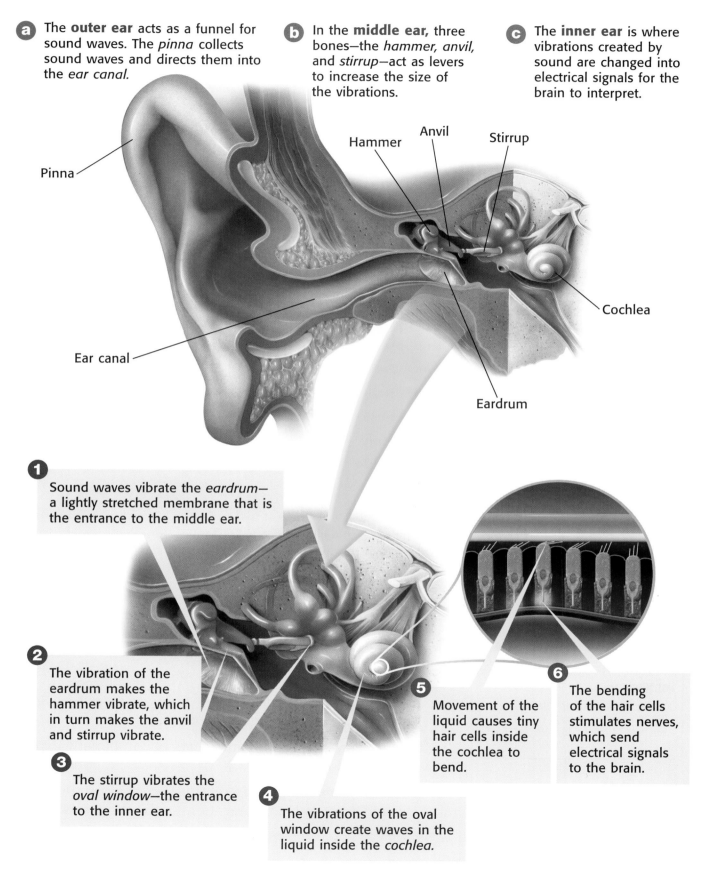

a The **outer ear** acts as a funnel for sound waves. The *pinna* collects sound waves and directs them into the *ear canal.*

b In the **middle ear**, three bones—the *hammer, anvil,* and *stirrup*—act as levers to increase the size of the vibrations.

c The **inner ear** is where vibrations created by sound are changed into electrical signals for the brain to interpret.

Hammer

Anvil

Stirrup

Pinna

Cochlea

Ear canal

Eardrum

1 Sound waves vibrate the *eardrum*—a lightly stretched membrane that is the entrance to the middle ear.

2 The vibration of the eardrum makes the hammer vibrate, which in turn makes the anvil and stirrup vibrate.

3 The stirrup vibrates the *oval window*—the entrance to the inner ear.

4 The vibrations of the oval window create waves in the liquid inside the *cochlea.*

5 Movement of the liquid causes tiny hair cells inside the cochlea to bend.

6 The bending of the hair cells stimulates nerves, which send electrical signals to the brain.

Could a dinosaur have played a horn? Check it out on page 58.

Hearing Loss and Deafness The many parts of the ear must work together for you to hear sounds. If any part of the ear is damaged or does not work properly, hearing loss or deafness may result.

One of the most common types of hearing loss is called *tinnitus* (ti NIE tuhs), which results from long-term exposure to loud sounds. Loud sounds can cause damage to the hair cells and nerve endings in the cochlea. Damage to the cochlea or any part of the inner ear usually results in permanent hearing loss.

People who have tinnitus often complain about hearing a ringing in their ears. They also have difficulties understanding other people and hearing the difference between words that sound very similar. Tinnitus can affect people of any age. Fortunately, tinnitus can be prevented. **Figure 5** shows some ways that you can protect yourself from hearing loss.

Figure 5 *Reducing exposure to loud sounds will protect your ears.*

Wearing ear protection while working with machinery blocks out some of the sounds that can injure your ears.

Turning your radio down will prevent hearing loss, especially when you use headphones.

SECTION REVIEW

1. Describe how a bell produces sound.

2. Explain why a person at a rock concert will not feel gusts of wind coming out of the speakers.

3. Name the three main parts of the ear, and briefly explain the function of each part.

4. **Inferring Conclusions** If a meteorite crashed on the moon, would you be able to hear it on Earth? Why or why not?

Terms to Learn

pitch   Doppler effect
infrasonic   loudness
ultrasonic   decibel

What You'll Do

◆ Compare the speed of sound in different media.
◆ Explain how frequency and pitch are related.
◆ Describe the Doppler effect, and give examples of it.
◆ Explain how amplitude and loudness are related.

Properties of Sound

Imagine you are swimming in a neighborhood pool. You hear many different sounds as you float on the water. Some are high, like the laughter of small children, and some are low, like the voices of men. Some sounds are loud, like the *BOING* of the diving board, and some are soft, like the sound of water lapping on the sides of the pool. The differences between the sounds—how high or low and how loud or soft they are—depend on the properties of the sound waves. In this section, you will learn about properties of sound.

The Speed of Sound Depends on the Medium

If two people at the other end of the pool shout at you at the same time, will you hear one person's voice before the other? No—the sounds of their voices will reach you at the same time. The time it takes for the sounds to reach you does not depend on who shouted or how loudly the person shouted. The speed of sound depends only on the medium through which the sound is traveling. Assuming that your head is above water, the sounds of the voices traveled through air to your ears and therefore traveled at the same speed.

Speed Changes When the Medium Changes The speed of sound through any medium is constant if the properties of the medium do not change. The chart at left shows the speed of sound in different media. If the properties of a medium change, the speed of sound through that medium will change. On the next page, you will explore how a change in one property—temperature—affects the speed of sound through air.

Speed of Sound in Different Media at 20°C	
Medium	**Speed (m/s)**
Air	343
Helium	1,005
Water	1,482
Sea water	1,522
Wood (oak)	3,850
Glass	4,540
Steel	5,200

Speed of Sound

The speed of sound depends on the medium through which sound is traveling and the medium's temperature. Sound travels at 343 m/s through air that has a temperature of 20°C. How far will sound travel in 3 seconds through air at 20°C?

$$\text{distance} = \text{speed} \times \text{time}$$

$$\text{distance} = 343\,\frac{m}{\not{s}} \times 3\,\not{s}$$

$$\text{distance} = 1{,}029\ m$$

Now It's Your Turn

How far does sound travel in 5 seconds through air, water, and steel at 20°C? Use the speeds given in the chart on the previous page.

The Speed of Sound Depends on Temperature In 1947, American pilot Chuck Yeager became the first person to travel faster than the speed of sound. But he was flying at a speed of only 293 m/s! If the speed of sound in air is 343 m/s (as shown in the chart on the previous page), how did Yeager fly faster than the speed of sound? The answer has to do with the temperature of the air.

In general, the cooler the medium, the slower the speed of sound. This happens because particles in cool materials move slower than particles in warmer materials. When the particles move slower, they transmit energy more slowly. Therefore, sound travels more slowly in cold air than in hot air.

Chuck Yeager flew at 12,000 m above sea level. At that height the temperature of the air is so low that the speed of sound is only 290 m/s. So when he flew at 293 m/s, he was flying 3 m/s faster than the speed of sound.

Pitch Depends on Frequency

Think about the guitar you made at the beginning of this chapter. You used two rubber bands of different thicknesses as strings. You probably noticed that the thicker rubber band made a lower sound than the thinner rubber band made. How low or high you perceive a sound to be is the **pitch** of that sound.

The pitch of a sound is determined by the frequency of the sound wave, as shown in **Figure 6**. The *frequency* of a wave is the number of waves produced in a given time. Frequency is expressed in *hertz* (Hz), where 1 Hz = 1 wave per second.

Figure 6 *The thicker tuning fork vibrates at a lower frequency. Therefore, it creates a sound with a lower pitch.*

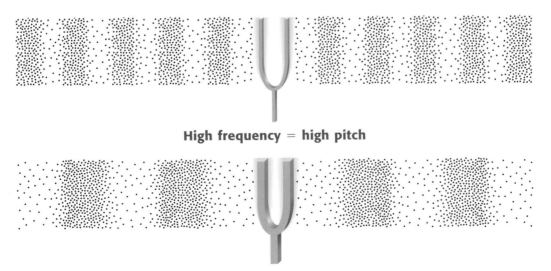

High frequency = high pitch

Low frequency = low pitch

Frequency and Hearing Some people use dog whistles to call their dog. But when you see someone blow a dog whistle, the whistle seems silent to you. That's because the frequency of the sound wave is out of the range of human hearing. But the dog hears a very high pitch from the whistle and comes running! The graph below compares the range of frequencies that humans and animals can hear.

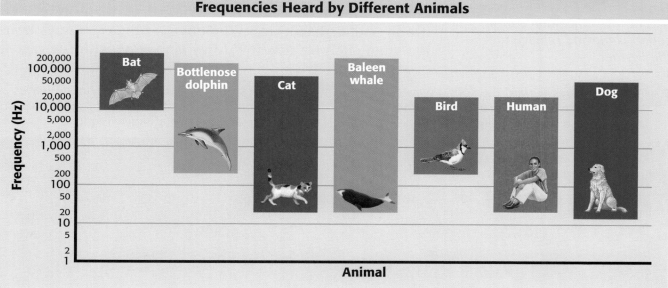

Frequencies Heard by Different Animals

Frequencies You Can Hear The average human ear can detect sounds that have frequencies between 20 Hz and 20,000 Hz. Examples of sounds within this range include the lowest sound a pipe organ can make (about 40 Hz) and the screech of a bat (10,000 Hz or higher). The range of hearing varies from person to person. Young children can often hear sounds with frequencies above this range, while many elderly people have difficulty hearing sounds higher than 8,000 Hz.

Frequencies You Can't Hear Sounds that are outside the range of human hearing have special names. Sounds with frequencies that are lower than 20 Hz are described as **infrasonic.** Sounds with frequencies that are higher than 20,000 Hz are described as **ultrasonic.** The sounds are given these names because *sonic* refers to sound, *infra* means "below," and *ultra* means "beyond."

Ultrasonic waves have a variety of applications. For example, ultrasonic waves are used to clean jewelry and to remove ice from metal. Scientists hope to use this technology to remove ice from airplane wings, car windshields, and freezers. You will learn about other uses of ultrasonic waves in the next section.

Biology

C O N N E C T I O N

Kidney stones—deposits of calcium salts that form inside kidneys—can cause a great deal of pain. Sometimes they are so large that they have to be removed by a doctor. Surgery was once the primary way to remove kidney stones, but now ultrasonic waves can be used to break kidney stones into smaller pieces that can pass out of the body with urine.

The Doppler Effect Have you ever been passed by a car with its horn honking? If so, you probably noticed the sudden change in pitch—sort of an *EEEEEOOooooowwn* sound—as the car sped past you. The pitch you heard was higher while the car was approaching than it was after the car passed. This is a result of the Doppler effect. For sound waves, the **Doppler effect** is the apparent change in the frequency of a sound caused by the motion of either the listener or the source of the sound. **Figure 7** explains the Doppler effect. Keep in mind that the frequency of the car horn does not really change; it only sounds like it does. The driver of the car always hears the same pitch because the driver is moving with the car.

Figure 7 *The Doppler effect occurs when the source of a sound is moving relative to the listener.*

ⓐ The car moves toward the sound waves in front of it, causing the waves to be closer together and to have a higher frequency.

ⓑ The car moves away from the sound waves behind it, causing the waves to be farther apart and to have a lower frequency.

ⓒ A listener in front of the car hears a higher pitch than a listener behind the car.

Loudness Is Related to Amplitude

If you gently tap a bass drum, you will hear a soft rumbling. But if you strike the drum with a large force, you will hear a loud *BOOM*! By changing the force you use to strike the drum, you change the loudness of the sound that is created. **Loudness** is how loud or soft a sound is perceived to be.

Energy and Vibration The harder you strike a drum, the louder the boom. As you strike the drum harder, you transfer more energy to the drum. The drum moves with a larger vibration and transfers more energy to the surrounding air. This increase in energy causes air particles to vibrate farther from their rest positions.

Increasing Amplitude When you strike a drum harder, you are increasing the amplitude of the sound waves being created. The *amplitude* of a wave is the maximum distance the particles in a wave vibrate from their rest positions. The larger the amplitude, the louder the sound, and the smaller the amplitude, the softer the sound. **Figure 8** shows one way to increase the loudness of a sound. Do the QuickLab on this page to investigate the loudness and pitch of sounds.

Figure 8 *An amplifier increases the amplitude of the sound generated by an electric guitar.*

Measuring Loudness The most common unit used to express loudness is the **decibel (dB).** The faintest sounds an average human ear can hear are at a level of 0 dB. The level of 120 dB is sometimes called the threshold of pain because sounds at that level and higher can cause your ears to hurt. Continued exposure to sounds above 85 dB causes gradual hearing loss by permanently damaging the hair cells in your inner ear. The chart below shows the decibel levels of some common sounds.

Some Common Decibel Levels	
Sound	**Decibel level**
The softest sounds you can hear	0
Whisper	20
Purring cat	25
Normal conversation	60
Lawn mower, vacuum cleaner, truck traffic	80
Chain saw, snowmobile	100
Sandblaster, loud rock concert, automobile horn	115
Threshold of pain	120
Jet engine 30 m away	140
Rocket engine 50 m away	200

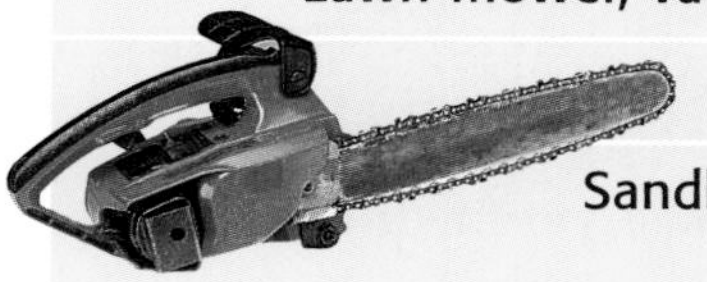

QuickLab

Sounding Board

1. With one hand, hold a **metric ruler** on your desk so that one end of it hangs over the edge.

2. With your other hand, pull the free end of the ruler up a few centimeters and let go.

3. Try pulling the ruler up different distances. How does the distance affect the sounds you hear? What property of the sound wave are you changing?

4. Try changing the length of the part that hangs over the edge. What property of the sound wave is affected?

5. Record your answers and observations in your ScienceLog.

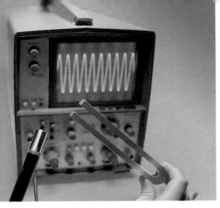

Figure 9 *An oscilloscope can be used to represent sounds.*

"Seeing" Sounds Because sound waves are invisible, their amplitude and frequency is impossible to measure directly. However, technology can provide a way to "see" sound waves. A device called an *oscilloscope* (uh SIL uh sкoнp), shown in **Figure 9,** is used to graph representations of sound waves.

A microphone first converts the sound wave into an electric current. The oscilloscope then converts the electric current into graphs such as the ones shown in **Figure 10.** Notice that the graphs look like transverse waves instead of longitudinal waves. The highest points (crests) of these waves represent compressions, and the lowest points (troughs) represent rarefactions. By looking at the displays on the oscilloscope, you can quickly see the difference in both amplitude and frequency of sound waves.

Figure 10 "Seeing" Sounds

The graph on the right has a **larger amplitude** than the graph on the left. Therefore, the sound represented on the right is **louder** than the one on the left.

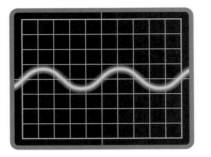
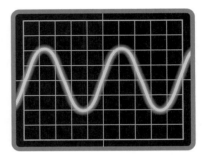

The graph on the right has a **lower frequency** than the one on the left. So the sound represented on the right has a **lower pitch** than the one on the left.

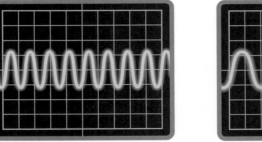
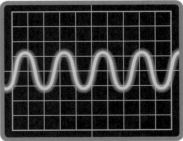

internetconnect

*SCi*LINKS.
NSTA

TOPIC: Properties of Sound
GO TO: www.scilinks.org
*sci*LINKS NUMBER: HSTP515

SECTION REVIEW

1. In general, how does changing the temperature of a medium affect the speed of sound through that medium?

2. What properties of waves affect the pitch and loudness of sound?

3. **Inferring Conclusions** Will a listener notice the Doppler effect if he or she and the source of the sound are traveling toward each other? Explain your answer.

Terms to Learn

reflection   sonic boom
echo   standing wave
echolocation   resonance
interference   diffraction

What You'll Do

◆ Explain how echoes are produced, and describe their use in locating objects.
◆ Give examples of constructive and destructive interference of sound waves.
◆ Identify three sound-wave interactions, and give examples of each.

Interactions of Sound Waves

Beluga whales, such as those shown in **Figure 11,** communicate by using a wide variety of sounds, including clicks, chirps, whistles, trills, screeches, and moos. The sounds they make can be heard above and below water. Because of the wide range of sounds they make, belugas have been nicknamed "sea canaries." But belugas use sound for more than just communication—they also use reflected sound waves to find fish, crabs, and shrimp to eat. In this section you'll learn about reflection and other interactions of sound waves.

Figure 11 *Beluga whales depend on sound interactions for survival.*

Reflection of Sound Waves

Reflection is the bouncing back of a wave after it strikes a barrier. You're probably already familiar with a reflected sound wave, otherwise known as an **echo.** The amount a sound wave will reflect depends on the reflecting surface. Sound waves reflect best off smooth, hard surfaces. That's why a shout in an empty gymnasium can produce an echo, but a shout in an empty auditorium usually does not, as shown in **Figure 12.**

Figure 12
Sound Reflection and Absorption

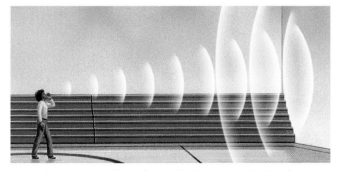

Sound waves easily reflect off the smooth, hard walls of a gymnasium. That's why you hear an echo.

In well-designed auditoriums, echoes are reduced by soft materials that absorb sound waves and by irregular shapes that scatter sound waves.

Echolocation Beluga whales use echoes to find food. The process of using reflected sound waves to find objects is called **echolocation**. Other animals—such as dolphins, bats, and some species of birds—also use echolocation to hunt food and detect objects in their paths. **Figure 13** shows how echolocation works.

Figure 13 *Bats use echolocation to navigate around barriers and to find insects to eat.*

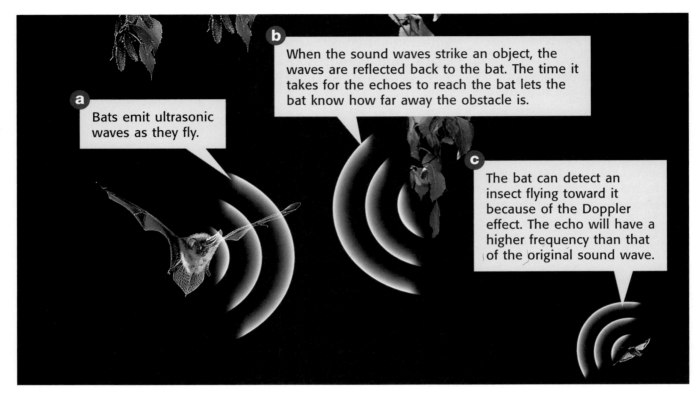

a Bats emit ultrasonic waves as they fly.

b When the sound waves strike an object, the waves are reflected back to the bat. The time it takes for the echoes to reach the bat lets the bat know how far away the obstacle is.

c The bat can detect an insect flying toward it because of the Doppler effect. The echo will have a higher frequency than that of the original sound wave.

Echolocation Technology Humans use echoes to locate objects underwater and underground by using sonar (**so**und **na**vigation **a**nd **r**anging). *Sonar* is a type of electronic echolocation. **Figure 14** shows how sonar works. Ultrasonic waves are used because their short wavelengths provide more details about the objects they reflect off. Sonar can also help navigators on ships detect icebergs and can help oceanographers map the ocean floor.

Figure 14 *A depth finder sends ultrasonic waves down into the water. The time it takes for the echo to return helps the fishermen determine the location of the fish.*

Insightful Technology

Many people who are blind use a cane to help them detect obstacles while they are walking. Now engineers have developed a sonar cane, shown at right, to help blind people even more. The cane emits and detects sound waves. Based on your knowledge of echolocation, explain how you think this cane works.

Ultrasonography Another type of electronic echolocation is used in a medical procedure called *ultrasonography*. Ultrasonography uses echoes to "see" inside a patient's body without performing surgery. A device called a transducer produces ultrasonic waves, which reflect off the patient's internal organs. These echoes are then converted into images that can be seen on a television monitor, as shown in **Figure 15.** Ultrasonography is used to examine kidneys, gallbladders, and other abdominal organs and to check the development of an unborn baby in a mother's body. Ultrasonic waves are safer than X rays because sound waves are less harmful to human tissue.

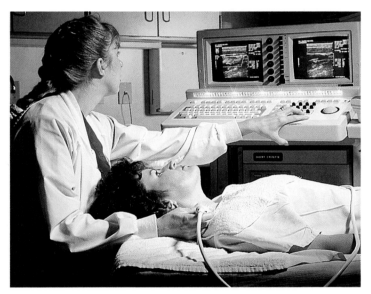

Figure 15 *Images created by ultrasonography are fuzzy, but they are a safe way to see inside a patient's body.*

SECTION REVIEW

1. Describe a place in which you would expect to hear echoes.

2. How do bats use echoes to find insects to eat?

3. **Comparing Concepts** Explain how sonar and ultrasonography are similar when used to locate objects.

Interference of Sound Waves

Another interaction of sound waves is interference. **Interference** is the result of two or more waves overlapping. **Figure 16** shows how two sound waves can combine by both constructive and destructive interference.

Figure 16 *Sound waves from two speakers producing sound of the same frequency combine by both constructive and destructive interference.*

Constructive Interference
As the compressions of one wave overlap the compressions of another wave, the sound will be louder because the amplitude is increased.

Destructive Interference
As the compressions of one wave overlap the rarefactions of another wave, the sound will be softer because the amplitude is decreased.

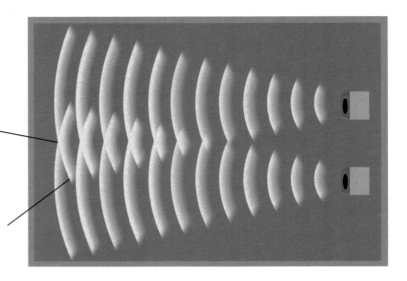

Orchestras and bands take advantage of constructive interference when several instruments play the same notes. The sound waves from the instruments combine by constructive interference to produce a louder sound. But destructive interference may keep you from hearing the concert. "Dead spots" are areas in an auditorium where sound waves reflecting off the walls interfere destructively with the sound waves from the stage. If you are at a concert and you can't hear the orchestra very well, try changing seats before you decide to get your ears checked!

Constructive interference

The Sound Barrier   As the source of a sound—such as a jet plane—accelerates to the speed of sound, the sound waves in front of the jet plane compress closer and closer together. **Figure 17** shows what happens as a jet plane reaches the speed of sound.

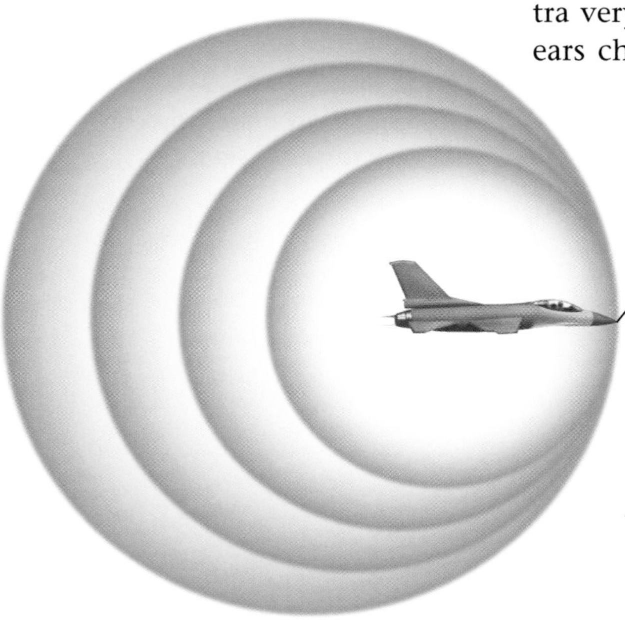

Figure 17 *When a jet plane reaches the speed of sound, the sound waves in front of the jet combine by constructive interference. The result is a high-density compression that is called the sound barrier.*

Shock Waves and Sonic Booms For the jet in Figure 17 to travel faster than the speed of sound, it must overcome the pressure of the compressed sound waves. **Figure 18** shows what happens as soon as the jet achieves supersonic speeds—speeds faster than the speed of sound. At these speeds, the sound waves trail off behind the jet and combine at their outer edges to form a shock wave.

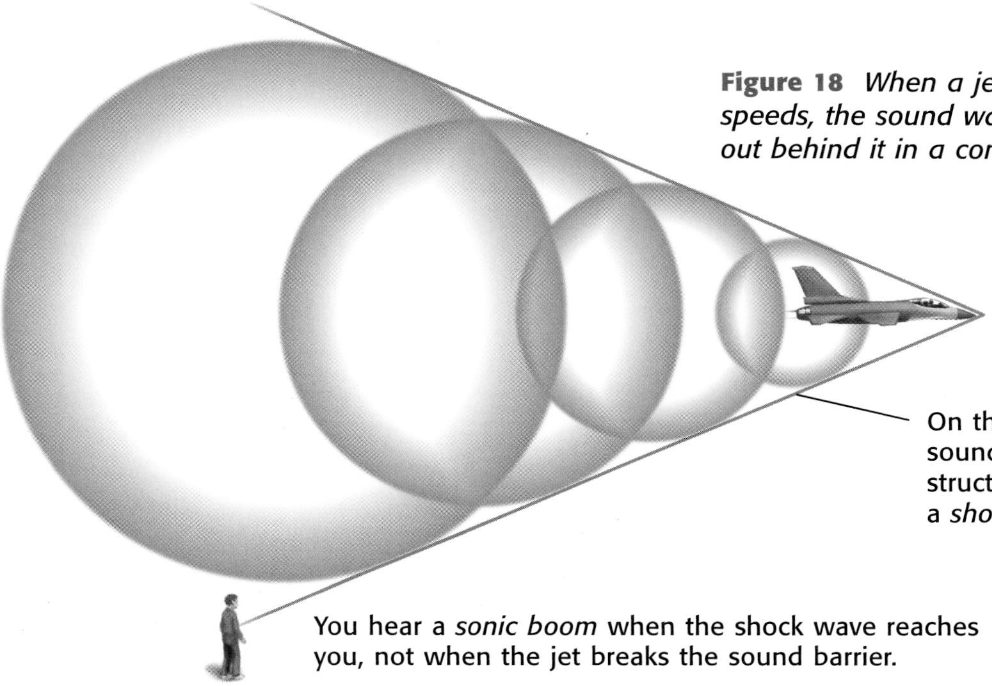

Figure 18 *When a jet travels at supersonic speeds, the sound waves it creates spread out behind it in a cone shape.*

On the edge of the cone, the sound waves combine by constructive interference to produce a *shock wave*.

You hear a *sonic boom* when the shock wave reaches you, not when the jet breaks the sound barrier.

A **sonic boom** is the explosive sound heard when a shock wave reaches your ears. Sonic booms can be so loud that they can hurt your ears and break windows. They can even make the ground shake as it does during an earthquake.

✔ Self-Check

Explain why two people will not hear a sonic boom at the same time if they are standing a block or two apart. *(See page 152 to check your answer.)*

BRAIN FOOD

The cracking sound made by a whip is actually a miniature sonic boom caused by the shock wave formed as the tip of the whip travels faster than the speed of sound!

Standing Waves When you play a guitar, you can make some pleasing sounds and maybe even play a tune. But have you ever watched a guitar string after you've plucked it? You may have noticed that the string vibrates as a standing wave. A **standing wave** is a result of interference in which portions of the wave are at the rest position and other portions have a large amplitude.

Resonant Frequencies Although you can see only one standing wave, the guitar string actually creates several standing waves of different frequencies at the same time. The frequencies at which standing waves are made are called *resonant frequencies*. Resonant frequencies are sometimes called by special names, as shown in **Figure 19.**

Figure 19 *A plucked string vibrates at several resonant frequencies.*

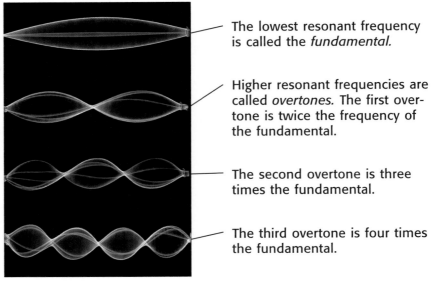

The lowest resonant frequency is called the *fundamental.*

Higher resonant frequencies are called *overtones.* The first overtone is twice the frequency of the fundamental.

The second overtone is three times the fundamental.

The third overtone is four times the fundamental.

LabBook

A tuning fork and a plastic tube make beautiful music together on page 131 of the LabBook.

Resonance Would you believe that you can make a guitar string make a sound without touching it? You can do this if you have a tuning fork, shown in **Figure 20,** that vibrates at one of the resonant frequencies of the guitar string. Strike the tuning fork, and hold it close to the string. The string will start to vibrate and produce a sound. The effect is the greatest when the resonant frequency of the tuning fork matches the fundamental frequency of the string.

Using the vibrations of the tuning fork to make the string vibrate is an example of resonance. **Resonance** occurs when an object vibrating at or near a resonant frequency of a second object causes the second object to vibrate.

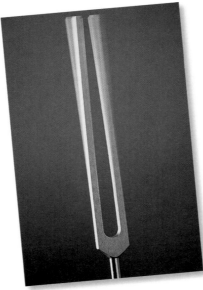

Figure 20 *When struck, a tuning fork can make certain objects vibrate.*

Diffraction of Sound Waves

Have you ever noticed the different sounds of thunder? From a distance, thunder sounds like a low rumbling. From nearby, thunder sounds like a loud *CRACK*! A type of wave interaction called diffraction causes this difference. **Diffraction** is the bending of waves around barriers or through openings. It is how sound waves travel around the corners of buildings and through doorways. The amount of diffraction is greatest when the size of the barrier or the opening is the same size or smaller than the wavelength of the sound waves, as shown in **Figure 21.**

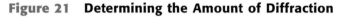
Figure 21   Determining the Amount of Diffraction

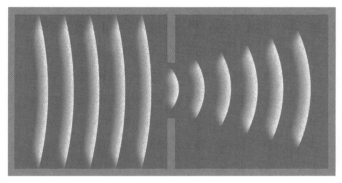

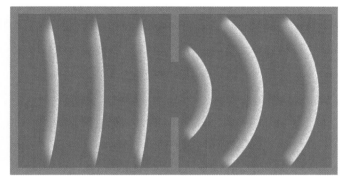

High-frequency sound waves have short wavelengths and do not diffract very much when they travel through a doorway. Therefore, high pitches can be hard to hear when you are in the next room.

Low-frequency sound waves have longer wavelengths, so they diffract more through doorways. Therefore, you can hear lower pitches better when you are in the next room.

So what about thunder? Thunder consists of both high- and low-frequency sound waves. When lightning strikes nearby, you hear all the sound waves together as a loud cracking noise. But when the lightning strikes far away, buildings, trees, hills, and other barriers stop most of the high-frequency waves. Only the low-frequency waves can diffract around these large objects, and thus you hear only a low rumbling.

SECTION REVIEW

1. How is a sound barrier formed?

2. When you are in a classroom, why can you hear voices from the hallway even when you cannot see who is talking?

3. **Inferring Conclusions**   Your friend is playing a song on a piano. Whenever your friend hits a certain key, the lamp on top of the piano rattles. Explain why this happens.

Terms to Learn

sound quality
noise

What You'll Do

- Define sound quality.
- Describe how each family of musical instruments produces sound.
- Explain how noise is different from music.

Sound Quality

Have you ever been told that some music you really like is just a lot of noise? If you have, you know that people sometimes disagree about the difference between noise and music. You probably think of noise as sounds you don't like and think of music as sounds that are interesting and pleasant to hear. But there is actually a difference between music and noise, and the difference has to do with sound quality.

What Is Sound Quality?

If the same note is played with the same loudness on a piano and on a violin, could you tell the instruments apart without looking? Although the notes played are identical, you probably could tell them apart because the sounds the instruments produce are not the same. The notes sound different because each instrument actually produces several different pitches: the fundamental and several overtones. These pitches are modeled in **Figure 22.** The result of several pitches blending together through interference is **sound quality.** Each instrument has a unique sound quality. **Figure 23** shows how the sound quality differs when two instruments play the same note.

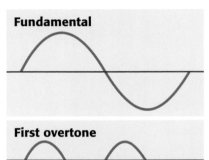
Fundamental

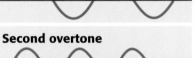
First overtone

Second overtone

Resulting sound

Figure 22 *The top three diagrams represent three different pitches played at the same time. The bottom diagram shows the result when the pitches blend through interference.*

Figure 23 *An oscilloscope shows the difference in sound quality of the same note played on different instruments.*

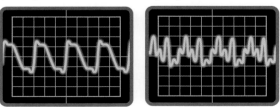

Piano   **Violin**

Sound Quality of Instruments

When you listen to an orchestra play you can hear many different kinds of instruments. The difference in sound quality among the instruments comes from the structural differences of the instruments. All instruments produce sound with vibrations. But the part of the instrument that vibrates and how the vibrations are made vary from instrument to instrument. Even so, all instruments fall within three main families: string instruments, wind instruments, and percussion instruments.

✓ Self-Check

Which wave interaction is most important in determining sound quality? *(See page 152 to check your answer.)*

String Instruments Violins, guitars, and banjos are examples of string instruments. They produce sound when their strings vibrate after being plucked or bowed. **Figure 24** shows how two different string instruments produce sounds.

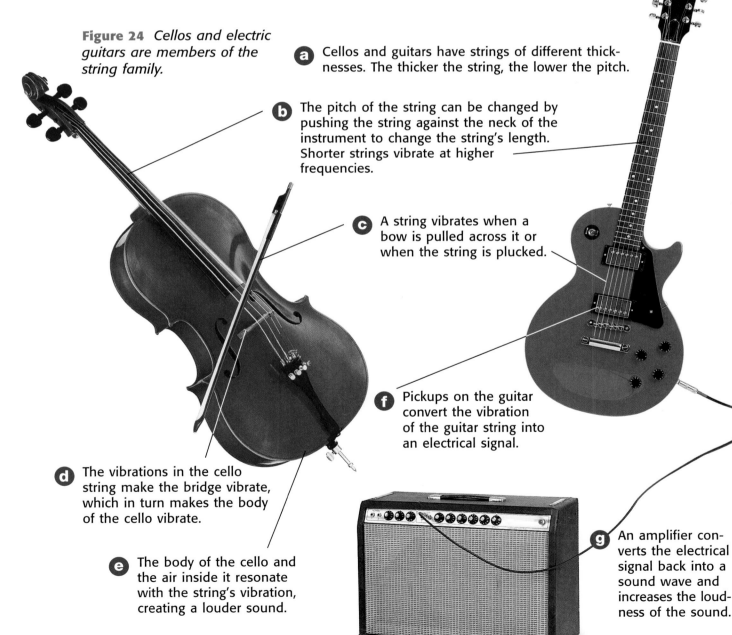

Figure 24 *Cellos and electric guitars are members of the string family.*

a Cellos and guitars have strings of different thicknesses. The thicker the string, the lower the pitch.

b The pitch of the string can be changed by pushing the string against the neck of the instrument to change the string's length. Shorter strings vibrate at higher frequencies.

c A string vibrates when a bow is pulled across it or when the string is plucked.

f Pickups on the guitar convert the vibration of the guitar string into an electrical signal.

d The vibrations in the cello string make the bridge vibrate, which in turn makes the body of the cello vibrate.

e The body of the cello and the air inside it resonate with the string's vibration, creating a louder sound.

g An amplifier converts the electrical signal back into a sound wave and increases the loudness of the sound.

Wind Instruments A wind instrument produces sound when a vibration is created at one end of its air column. The vibration creates standing waves in the air column. Wind instruments are sometimes divided into two groups—woodwinds and brass. Examples of woodwinds are saxophones, oboes, and recorders. Brass instruments include French horns, trombones, and tubas. A woodwind instrument and a brass instrument are shown in **Figure 25.**

Figure 25 *Clarinets are woodwind instruments, and trumpets are brass instruments.*

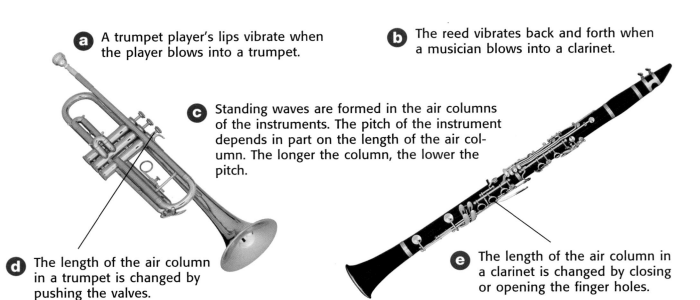

a A trumpet player's lips vibrate when the player blows into a trumpet.

b The reed vibrates back and forth when a musician blows into a clarinet.

c Standing waves are formed in the air columns of the instruments. The pitch of the instrument depends in part on the length of the air column. The longer the column, the lower the pitch.

d The length of the air column in a trumpet is changed by pushing the valves.

e The length of the air column in a clarinet is changed by closing or opening the finger holes.

Percussion Instruments Drums, bells, and cymbals are examples of percussion instruments. They produce sound when struck. Different-sized instruments are used to get different pitches. Usually, the larger the instrument, the lower the pitch. **Figure 26** shows examples of percussion instruments.

Figure 26 *Drums and cymbals in a trap set are examples of percussion instruments.*

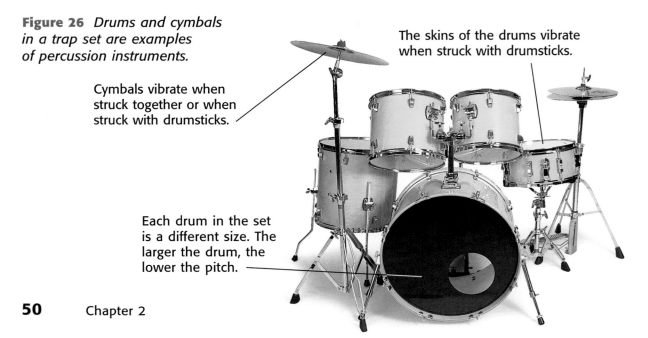

The skins of the drums vibrate when struck with drumsticks.

Cymbals vibrate when struck together or when struck with drumsticks.

Each drum in the set is a different size. The larger the drum, the lower the pitch.

Music or Noise?

Most of the sounds we hear are noises. The sound of a truck roaring down the highway, the slamming of a door, and the jingle of keys falling to the floor are all noises. **Noise** can be described as any undesired sound, especially a nonmusical sound, that includes a random mix of pitches. **Figure 27** shows the difference between a musical sound and noise on an oscilloscope.

Figure 27 *A note from a French horn produces a sound wave with a repeating pattern, but noise from a clap produces complex sound waves with no pattern.*

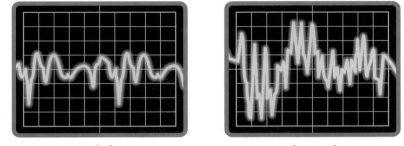

| French horn | A sharp clap |

Noise Pollution The amount of noise around you can become so great that it is not only bothersome but can cause health problems. When noise reaches a level that causes pain or damages the body, it is considered *noise pollution*.

Noise pollution can damage the inner ear, causing permanent hearing loss. Noise pollution can also contribute to sleeplessness, high blood pressure, and stress. Because of these health concerns, the federal government has set noise exposure limits for people who work in areas with loud noises. Noise pollution also makes the environment less livable for humans as well as wildlife.

Environment
C O N N E C T I O N

The Los Angeles International Airport was built next to the main habitat of an endangered butterfly species called the El Segundo blue. The noise pollution from the airport has driven people and other animals from the area, but the butterflies are not affected because they have no ears!

SECTION REVIEW

1. What is the role of interference in determining sound quality?

2. Name the three families of musical instruments, and describe how vibrations are created in each family.

3. **Interpreting Graphics** Look at the oscilloscope screen at right. Do you think the sound represented by the wave on the screen was noise or music? Explain your answer.

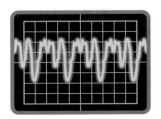

internetconnect

SciLINKS
NSTA

TOPIC: Sound Quality
GO TO: www.scilinks.org
*sci*LINKS NUMBER: HSTP525

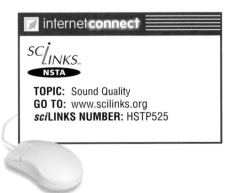

Skill Builder Lab

The Energy of Sound

In this chapter, you learned about properties and interactions of sound. In this lab, you will perform several activities that will show that the properties and interactions of sound all depend on one thing—the energy carried by sound waves.

MATERIALS

- 2 tuning forks of the same frequency and 1 of a different frequency
- pink rubber eraser
- small plastic cup filled with water
- rubber band
- piece of string, 50 cm long

Part A: Sound Vibrations

Procedure

1 Lightly strike a tuning fork with the eraser. Slowly place the prongs of the tuning fork in the plastic cup of water. Record your observations in your ScienceLog.

Analysis

2 How do your observations show that sound waves are carried through vibrations?

Part B: Resonance

Procedure

3 Strike a tuning fork with the eraser. Quickly pick up a second tuning fork in your other hand, and hold it about 30 cm from the first tuning fork.

4 Place the first tuning fork against your leg to stop its vibration. Listen closely to the second tuning fork. Record your observations, as well as the frequencies of the two tuning forks.

5 Repeat steps 3 and 4, using the remaining tuning fork as the second tuning fork.

Analysis

6 Explain why you can hear a sound from the second tuning fork when the frequencies of the tuning forks used are the same.

7 When using tuning forks of different frequencies, predict whether you would hear a sound from the second tuning fork if you strike the first tuning fork harder. Explain your reasoning.

Part C: Interference

Procedure

8 Using the two tuning forks with the same frequency, place a rubber band tightly over the prongs near the base of one tuning fork. Strike both tuning forks at the same time against the eraser. Hold a tuning fork 3 to 5 cm from each ear. If you cannot hear any differences, move the rubber band farther down on the prongs. Strike again. Record your observations in your ScienceLog.

Analysis

9 Did you notice the sound changing back and forth between loud and soft? A steady pattern like this is called a beat frequency. Infer how this changing pattern of loudness and softness is related to interference (both constructive and destructive).

Part D: The Doppler Effect

Procedure

10 Your teacher will tie the piece of string securely to the base of one tuning fork. Your teacher will then strike the tuning fork and will carefully swing the tuning fork in a circle overhead. Record your observations in your ScienceLog.

Analysis

11 Did the tuning fork make a different sound when your teacher was swinging it than when he or she was holding it? If yes, explain why.

12 Is the actual frequency of the tuning fork changing? Explain.

Draw Conclusions, Parts A–D

13 Explain how your observations from each part of this lab show that sound waves carry energy from one point to another through a vibrating medium.

Going Further
Particularly loud thunder can cause the windows of your room to rattle. How is this evidence that sound waves carry energy?

Chapter Highlights

SECTION 1

Vocabulary

wave *(p. 31)*
medium *(p. 32)*
outer ear *(p. 33)*
middle ear *(p. 33)*
inner ear *(p. 33)*

Section Notes

- All sounds are created by vibrations and travel as longitudinal waves.

- Sound waves require a medium through which to travel.

- Sound waves travel in all directions away from their source.

- The sounds you hear are converted into electrical impulses by your ears and then sent to your brain for interpretation.

- Exposure to loud sounds can cause hearing loss and tinnitus.

SECTION 2

Vocabulary

pitch *(p. 36)*
infrasonic *(p. 37)*
ultrasonic *(p. 37)*
Doppler effect *(p. 38)*
loudness *(p. 38)*
decibel *(p. 39)*

Section Notes

- The speed of sound depends on the medium through which the sound is traveling. Changes in temperature of the medium can affect the speed of sound.

- The pitch of a sound depends on frequency. High-frequency sounds are high-pitched, and low-frequency sounds are low-pitched.

- Humans can hear sounds with frequencies between 20 Hz and 20,000 Hz.

- The Doppler effect is the apparent change in frequency of a sound caused by the motion of either the listener or the source of the sound.

- The loudness of a sound increases as the amplitude increases. Loudness is expressed in decibels.

- An oscilloscope can be used to "see" sounds.

Labs

Easy Listening *(p. 128)*

☑ Skills Check

Math Concepts

THE SPEED OF SOUND The speed of sound depends on the medium through which the sound waves are traveling. The speed of sound through wood at 20°C is 3,850 m/s. The distance sound will travel through wood in 5 seconds can be calculated as follows:

$$\text{distance} = \text{speed} \times \text{time}$$
$$= 3,850 \, \tfrac{\text{m}}{\text{s}} \times 5 \, \text{s}$$
$$= 19,250 \text{ m}$$

Visual Understanding

HOW THE HUMAN EAR WORKS The human ear has several parts that are divided into three regions—the outer ear, the middle ear, and the inner ear. Study the diagram on page 33 to review how the ear works.

Vocabulary

reflection *(p. 41)*

echo *(p. 41)*

echolocation *(p. 42)*

interference *(p. 44)*

sonic boom *(p. 45)*

standing wave *(p. 45)*

resonance *(p. 46)*

diffraction *(p. 47)*

Section Notes

- Echoes are reflected sound waves.

- Some animals use echolocation to find food or navigate around objects. Sonar and ultrasonography are types of echolocation.

- Sound barriers and shock waves are created by interference. You hear a sonic boom when a shock wave reaches your ears.

- Standing waves form at an object's resonant frequencies.

- Resonance occurs when a vibrating object causes a second object to vibrate at one of its resonant frequencies.

- The bending of sound waves around barriers or through openings is called diffraction. The amount of diffraction depends on the wavelength of the waves as well as the size of the opening.

Labs

The Speed of Sound *(p. 130)*

Tuneful Tube *(p. 131)*

Vocabulary

sound quality *(p. 48)*

noise *(p. 51)*

Section Notes

- Different instruments have different sound qualities.

- The three families of instruments are strings, winds, and percussion.

- The sound quality of noise is not pleasing because it is a random mix of frequencies.

---

 internetconnect

GO TO: go.hrw.com

Visit the **HRW** Web site for a variety of learning tools related to this chapter. Just type in the keyword:

KEYWORD: HSTSND

 SCi**LINKS**ₛₘ

N S T A

GO TO: www.scilinks.org

Visit the **National Science Teachers Association** on-line Web site for Internet resources related to this chapter. Just type in the *sci*LINKS number for more information about the topic:

TOPIC: What Is Sound?	***sci*LINKS NUMBER:** HSTP505
TOPIC: The Ear	***sci*LINKS NUMBER:** HSTP510
TOPIC: Properties of Sound	***sci*LINKS NUMBER:** HSTP515
TOPIC: Interactions of Sound Waves	***sci*LINKS NUMBER:** HSTP520
TOPIC: Sound Quality	***sci*LINKS NUMBER:** HSTP525

Chapter Review

To complete the following sentences, choose the correct term from each pair of terms listed below:

1. Humans cannot hear __?__ waves because their frequencies are above the range of human hearing. (*infrasonic* or *ultrasonic*)

2. In the __?__, vibrations are converted to electrical signals for the brain to interpret. (*middle ear* or *inner ear*)

3. The __?__ of a sound wave depends on its amplitude. (*loudness* or *pitch*)

4. Reflected sound waves are called __?__. (*echoes* or *noise*)

5. Two different instruments playing the same note sound different because of __?__. (*echolocation* or *sound quality*)

UNDERSTANDING CONCEPTS

Multiple Choice

6. If a fire engine is traveling toward you, the Doppler effect will cause the siren to sound
   a. higher.
   b. lower.
   c. louder.
   d. softer.

7. The wave interaction most important for echolocation is
   a. reflection.
   b. interference.
   c. diffraction.
   d. resonance.

8. If two sound waves interfere constructively, you will hear
   a. a high-pitched sound.
   b. a softer sound.
   c. a louder sound.
   d. no change in sound.

9. You will hear a sonic boom when
   a. an object breaks the sound barrier.
   b. an object travels at supersonic speeds.
   c. a shock wave reaches your ears.
   d. the speed of sound is 290 m/s.

10. Instruments that produce sound when struck belong to which family?
    a. strings
    b. winds
    c. percussion
    d. none of the above

11. Resonance can occur when an object vibrates at another object's
    a. resonant frequency.
    b. fundamental frequency.
    c. second overtone frequency.
    d. All of the above

12. The amount of diffraction that a sound wave undergoes depends on
    a. the frequency of the wave.
    b. the amplitude of the wave.
    c. the size of the barrier.
    d. Both (a) and (c)

13. A technological device that can be used to "see" sound waves is a(n)
    a. oscilloscope.
    b. sonar.
    c. transducer.
    d. amplifier.

Short Answer

14. Describe how the Doppler effect helps a beluga whale determine whether a fish is moving away from it or toward it.

15. How is interference involved in forming a shock wave?

16. Briefly describe how the three parts of the ear work.

Concept Mapping

17. Use the following terms to create a concept map: sound, sound wave, pitch, loudness, decibel, hertz, frequency, amplitude.

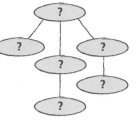

CRITICAL THINKING AND PROBLEM SOLVING

18. An anechoic chamber is a room where there is almost no reflection of sound waves. Anechoic chambers are often used to test sound equipment, such as stereos. The walls of such chambers are usually covered with foam triangles. Explain why this design eliminates echoes in the room.

19. Suppose you are sitting in the passenger seat of a parked car. You hear sounds coming from the stereo of another car parked on the opposite side of the street. You can easily hear the low-pitched bass sounds but cannot hear any high-pitched sounds coming from the parked car. Explain why you think this happens.

20. After working in a factory for a month, a man you know complains about a ringing in his ears. What might be wrong with him? What do you think may have caused his problem? What can you suggest to prevent further hearing loss?

MATH IN SCIENCE

21. How far does sound travel in 4 seconds through water at 20°C and glass at 20°C? Refer to the chart on page 35 for the speed of sound in different media.

INTERPRETING GRAPHICS

Use the oscilloscope screens below to answer the following questions:

22. Which sound is probably noise?

23. Which represents the softest sound?

24. Which represents the sound with the lowest pitch?

25. Which two sounds were produced by the same instrument?

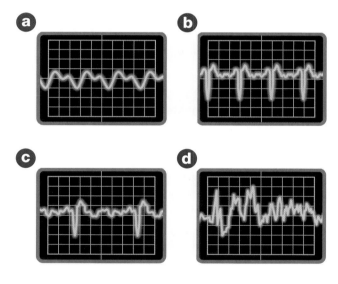

Reading Check-up

Take a minute to review your answers to the Pre-Reading Questions found at the bottom of page 28. Have your answers changed? If necessary, revise your answers based on what you have learned since you began this chapter.

Science, Technology, and Society

Jurassic Bark

Imagine you suddenly hear an incredibly loud honking sound, like a trombone or a tuba. "Must be band tryouts," you think. You turn to find the noise and find yourself face to face with a 10 m long, 2,800 kg dinosaur with a huge tubular crest extending back more than 2 m from its snout. Do you run? No—your musical friend, *Parasaurolophus,* is a vegetarian.

Now there's no way you'll bump into this extinct hadrosaur, a duck-billed dinosaur that existed about 75 million years ago in the late Cretaceous period. But through recent advances in computer technology, you can hear how *Parasaurolophus* might have sounded.

▶ *Aside from a role in the* Jurassic Park *movies, the* Parasaurolophus *dinosaur's biggest claim to fame is the enormous crest that extends back from its snout.*

A Snorkel or a Trombone?

Parasaurolophus's crest contained a network of tubes connected to the animal's breathing passages. Some scientists believe the dinosaurs used the distinctive crest to make sounds. Other scientists theorize that the crest allowed *Parasaurolophus* to stay underwater and feed, that it was used to regulate body temperature, or that it allowed the animals to communicate with each other by exhaling strongly through the crest.

The study of the *Parasaurolophus*'s potential sound-making ability really began after a 1995 expedition in northwestern New Mexico uncovered an almost-complete fossil skull of an adult. With this nearly complete skull and some modern technology, scientists tested the noise-making qualities of the crest.

Dino Scan

In Albuquerque, New Mexico, Dr. Carl Diegert of Sandia National Laboratories and Dr. Tom Williamson of the New Mexico Museum of Natural History and Science teamed up to use CT (Computed Tomography). With this scanning system, they created three-dimensional images of the crest's internal structure. The results showed that the crest had more tubes than previously thought as well as additional chambers.

Sound That Funky Horn

Once the crest's internal structure was determined, Diegert used powerful computers and special software to produce a sound that *Parasaurolophus* might have made. Since it is not known whether *Parasaurolophus* had vocal cords, Diegert made different versions of the sound by simulating the movement of air through the crest in several ways. Intrigued by Diegert's results, other researchers are trying to reproduce the sounds of other dinosaurs. In time, *Parasaurolophus* might be just one of a band of musical dinosaurs.

On Your Own

▶ *Parasaurolophus* is just one type of hadrosaur recognized for the peculiar bony crest on top of its head. On your own, research other hadrosaurs that had a bony crest similar to that of the *Parasaurolophus.* What are the names of these dinosaurs?

Science Fiction

"Ear"

by Jane Yolen

"Jily put on her Ear and sighed. The world went from awful silence to the pounding rhythms she loved. Without the Ear she was locked into her own thoughts and the few colors her eyes could pick out. But with the Ear she felt truly connected to the world."

Jily and her friends, Sanya and Feeny, live in a time not too far in the future. It is a time when everyone's hearing is damaged. People communicate using sign language—unless they put on their Ear. Then the whole world is filled with sounds. Of course, there are rules. No Ears allowed in school. Ears are only to be worn on the street, at night. Life is so much richer with an Ear, a person would have to be crazy to go without one.

The Low Down, the first club Jily and her friends visit, is too quiet for Jily's tastes. She wants to leave and tries to find Sanya and Feeny. But Sanya is dancing by herself, even though there is no music. When Jily finds Feeny, they notice some Earless kids their own age. Earless people never go to clubs, and Jily finds their presence offensive. But Feeny is intrigued.

Everyone is given an Ear at the age of 12 but has to give it up at the age of 30. Why would these kids want to go out without their Ears before the age of 30? Jily thinks the idea is ridiculous and doesn't stick around to find out the answer to such a question. But, it is an answer that will change her life by the end of the next day.

Read the rest of Jily's story, "Ear" by Jane Yolen, in the *Holt Anthology of Science Fiction*.

The Nature of Light

Pre-Reading
Questions

1. What is light?
2. How do light waves
   interact?
3. Why are you able to see
   different colors?

WHAT ON EARTH...?

What kind of alien life lives on *this* planet? Actually, this
isn't a planet at all. It's a photograph of something much,
much smaller. Have you guessed yet? It's an ordinary soap
bubble! The brightly colored swirls on the surface of this
bubble are reflections of light. In this chapter, you will
learn more about light, including how waves interact and
why you can see different colors like the ones on the surface of this soap bubble.

COLORS OF LIGHT

Is white light really white? In this activity, you will use a spectroscope to answer that question.

Procedure

1. Your teacher will give you a **spectroscope** or instructions for making one.

2. Turn on an **incandescent light bulb.** Look at the light bulb through your spectroscope. In your ScienceLog, write a description of what you see.

3. Repeat step 2 looking at a **fluorescent light.** Again, in your ScienceLog, describe what you see.

Analysis

4. Compare what you saw in step 2 with what you saw in step 3.

5. Both kinds of bulbs produce white light. What did you learn about white light using the spectroscope?

6. Light from the sun is white light. Make inferences about what you would see if you looked at sunlight using a spectroscope.
   Caution: Do NOT use your spectroscope to look at the sun. It does not give enough protection against bright sunlight.

Terms to Learn

electromagnetic wave
radiation

What You'll Do

◆ Explain why electromagnetic waves are transverse waves.
◆ Describe how electromagnetic waves are produced.
◆ Calculate distances traveled by light using the value for speed of light.

What Is Light?

We rely on light from the sun and from electric bulbs to help us see. But what exactly is light? Scientists are still studying light to learn more about its makeup and characteristics. Fortunately, much has already been discovered about light, as you will soon find out. You may even become enlightened!

Light Is an Electromagnetic Wave

Like sound, light is a type of energy that travels as a wave. But unlike sound, light does not require a medium through which to travel. Light is an **electromagnetic wave** (EM wave). An EM wave is a wave that can travel through space or matter and consists of changing electric and magnetic fields. A *field* is a region around an object that can exert a force, a push or pull, on another object without actually touching that object. For example, a magnet is surrounded by a magnetic field that can pull a paper clip toward it. But keep in mind that this field, like all fields, is not made of matter.

Figure 1 shows a diagram of an electromagnetic wave. Notice that the electric and magnetic fields are at right angles—or *perpendicular*—to each other. These fields are also perpendicular to the direction of the wave motion. Because of this arrangement, electromagnetic waves are transverse waves.

Figure 1 *Electromagnetic waves are transverse waves.*

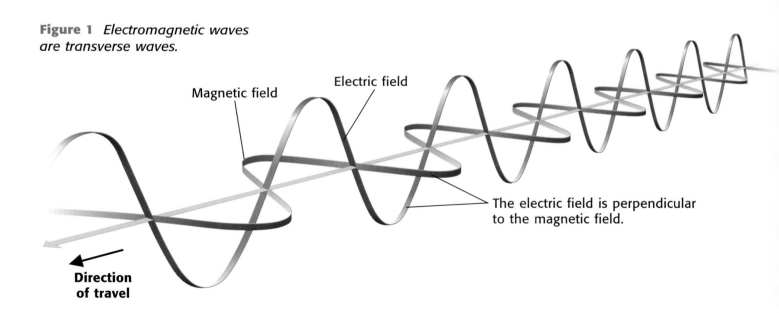

Magnetic field

Electric field

The electric field is perpendicular to the magnetic field.

Direction of travel

How Light Is Produced

An EM wave is produced by the vibration of an electrically charged particle. A particle with an electric charge is surrounded by an electric field. When the particle vibrates, or moves back and forth, the electric field around it vibrates too. When the electric field starts vibrating, a vibrating magnetic field is created. The vibration of an electric field and a magnetic field together produces an EM wave that carries energy released by the original vibration of the particle. The emission of energy in the form of EM waves is called **radiation.**

Sounds complicated, right? To better understand how light is produced, think about the following example. When you turn on a lamp, the electrical energy supplied to the filament in the bulb causes the atoms in the filament to vibrate. Charged particles inside the atoms then vibrate, and light is produced, as shown in **Figure 2.**

Extra! Extra! Read all about how light-producing fireflies save people's lives! Turn to page 90.

Figure 2 The Production of Light

a Electrons (negatively charged particles) in an atom move about the nucleus at different distances depending on the amount of energy they have. When an electron absorbs energy, it can jump to a new position.

b This new position is generally unstable, and the electron may not stay there very long. The electron returns to its original position, releasing the energy it absorbed in a tiny "packet" called a *photon.*

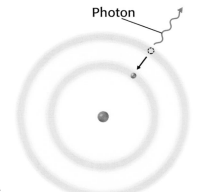

Nucleus

Electron

Photon

Energy levels

c The movement of electrons back and forth creates a stream of photons. This stream of photons can be thought of as waves of vibrating electric and magnetic fields. The stream of photons (the EM wave) carries the energy released by the electrons.

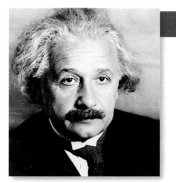

The Split Personality of Light

The fact that light is a wave explains certain behaviors of light, but not others. These puzzling behaviors of light are easier to explain if light is thought to consist of particles instead of waves. Scientists think that light has the properties of both a particle and a wave. Albert Einstein was one of many scientists who researched the dual nature of light. The idea that light can act as either particles or waves is known as the *particle-wave theory of light.*

The Nature of Light   **63**

The Speed of Light

Scientists have yet to discover anything in the universe that travels faster than light. In the near-vacuum of space, the speed of light is about 300,000,000 m/s. Light travels slightly slower in air, glass, and other types of matter. (Keep in mind that even though EM waves do not require a medium, they can travel through many substances.) Believe it or not, light can travel more than 880,000 times faster than sound! This explains the phenomenon described in **Figure 3.** And if you could run at the speed of light, you could travel around Earth 7.5 times in 1 second.

Figure 3 *Although thunder and lightning are produced at the same time, you usually see lightning before you hear thunder. That's because light travels much faster than sound.*

SECTION REVIEW

1. Why are electromagnetic waves transverse waves?

2. How is a sound wave different from an EM wave?

3. How does a charged particle produce an EM wave?

4. **Making Inferences** Explain why EM waves do not require a medium through which to travel.

5. **Doing Calculations** The distance from the sun to Jupiter is 778,000,000,000 m. How long does it take for light from the sun to reach Jupiter?

Terms to Learn

electromagnetic spectrum

What You'll Do

- ◆ Identify how EM waves differ from each other.
- ◆ Describe some uses for radio waves and microwaves.
- ◆ Give examples of how infrared waves and visible light are important in your life.
- ◆ Explain how ultraviolet light, X rays, and gamma rays can be both helpful and harmful.

The Electromagnetic Spectrum

When you look around, you can see objects because light reflects off them. But if a bee looked at the same objects, it would see them differently, as shown in **Figure 4.** This is because bees can see a kind of light that you can't see. This type of light is called ultraviolet light.

It might seem strange to you to call something you can't see *light,* because the light you are most familiar with is visible light. But ultraviolet light is very similar to visible light. Both visible light and ultraviolet light are types of EM waves. In this section you will learn about many other types of EM waves, including X rays, radio waves, and microwaves.

Figure 4 *The petals of the flower on the right look solid yellow to you. But a bee may see dark ultraviolet markings that make the same flower appear quite different to the bee.*

Astronomy CONNECTION

Scientists know that all electromagnetic waves in empty space travel at the same speed. If EM waves traveled at different speeds, planets, stars, and galaxies would appear to be in different places depending upon which EM wave was used to view them. For example, using X rays to view a star might make the star appear to be in a different place than if radio waves were used.

Characteristics of EM Waves

Even though there are many types of EM waves, each type of wave travels at the same speed in a vacuum—300,000,000 m/s. How is this possible? Well, the speed of a wave is determined by multiplying its wavelength by its frequency. So EM waves having different wavelengths can travel at the same speed as long as their frequencies are also different. The entire range of EM waves is called the **electromagnetic spectrum.** Categories of waves in the EM spectrum include radio waves, microwaves, and visible light.

Radio Waves

Radio waves cover a wide range of waves in the EM spectrum. Radio waves have some of the longest wavelengths and the lowest frequencies of all EM waves. Therefore, radio waves are low energy waves. They carry enough energy, however, to be used for broadcasting radio signals. **Figure 5** shows how this process works.

Radio stations encode sound information into radio waves by varying either the waves' amplitude or their frequency. Changing amplitude or frequency is called modulation. You probably know that there are AM radio stations and FM radio stations. The abbreviation AM stands for amplitude modulation, and the abbreviation FM stands for frequency modulation. AM radio waves have longer wavelengths than FM radio waves.

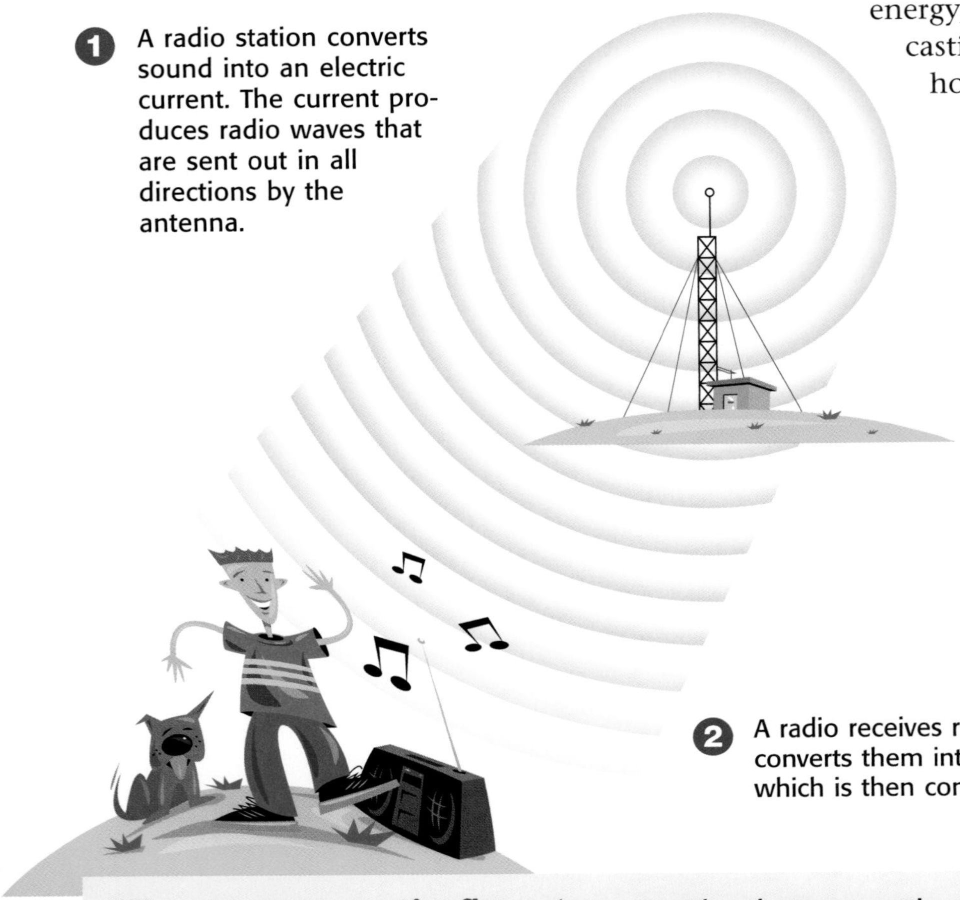

Figure 5 *Radio waves cannot be heard, but they carry energy that can be converted into sound.*

1 A radio station converts sound into an electric current. The current produces radio waves that are sent out in all directions by the antenna.

2 A radio receives radio waves and then converts them into an electric current, which is then converted to sound.

Electromagnetic Spectrum

The electromagnetic spectrum is arranged from long to short wavelength or from low to high frequency.

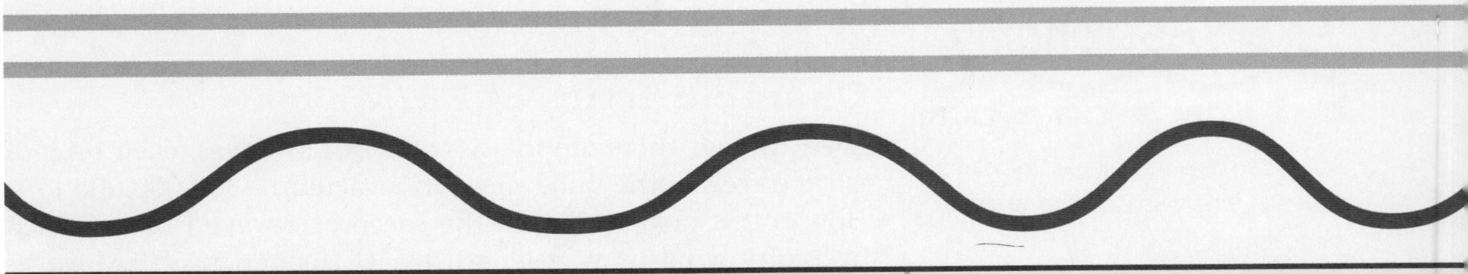

Radio waves	Microwaves	Infrared
All radio and television stations broadcast radio waves.	Despite their name, microwaves are not the shortest EM waves.	*Infrared* means "below red."

AM and FM Radio Waves Although AM radio waves can travel farther than FM waves, as shown in **Figure 6,** many stations—especially those that broadcast mostly music—use FM waves. That's because more information can be encoded by using frequency modulation than by using amplitude modulation. Because FM waves carry more information, music broadcast from FM stations sounds better.

Figure 6 *The difference in the wavelengths of AM and FM radio waves affects how the waves interact with a layer of the atmosphere called the ionosphere.*

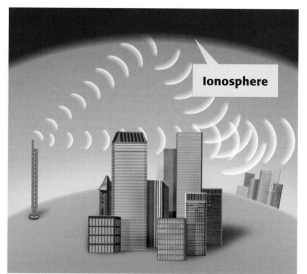

AM radio waves can reflect off the ionosphere. This helps AM waves travel long distances.

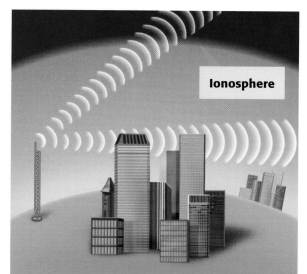

FM radio waves pass through the ionosphere. Therefore, FM waves cannot travel as far as AM waves.

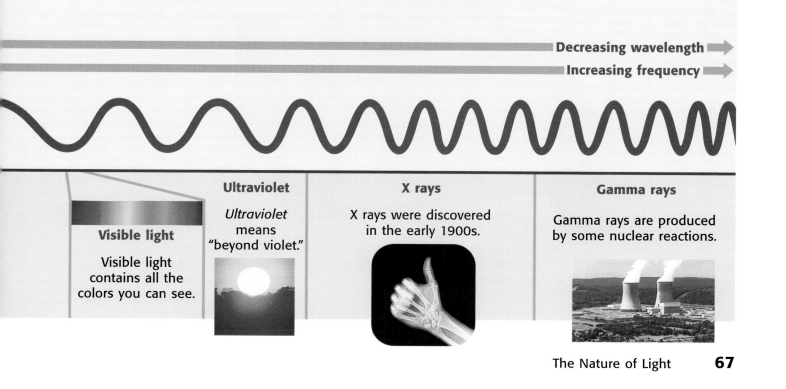

Decreasing wavelength ⟹
Increasing frequency ⟹

Visible light

Visible light contains all the colors you can see.

Ultraviolet

Ultraviolet means "beyond violet."

X rays

X rays were discovered in the early 1900s.

Gamma rays

Gamma rays are produced by some nuclear reactions.

Television and Radio Waves Television signals are also carried by radio waves. Most television stations broadcast radio waves that have shorter wavelengths and higher frequencies than those broadcast by radio stations. However, television signals are still broadcast using amplitude modulation and frequency modulation. Television stations use frequency-modulated waves to carry sound and amplitude-modulated waves to carry pictures.

Some waves carrying television signals are transmitted to satellites around the Earth. The waves are amplified and relayed back to ground antennae and then travel through cables to televisions in homes. This is how cable television works.

Microwaves

Microwaves have shorter wavelengths and higher frequencies than radio waves. Therefore, microwaves carry more energy than radio waves. You are probably familiar with microwaves—they are created in a microwave oven, like the model illustrated in **Figure 7.**

Figure 7 How a Microwave Oven Works

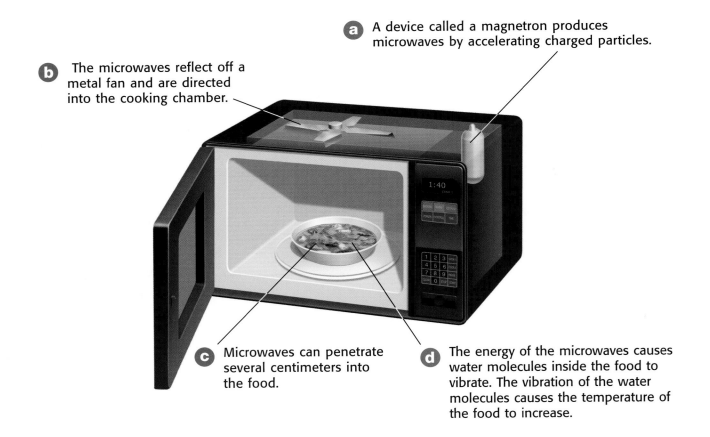

a A device called a magnetron produces microwaves by accelerating charged particles.

b The microwaves reflect off a metal fan and are directed into the cooking chamber.

c Microwaves can penetrate several centimeters into the food.

d The energy of the microwaves causes water molecules inside the food to vibrate. The vibration of the water molecules causes the temperature of the food to increase.

Radar Microwaves are also used in radar. Radar (**ra**dio **d**etection **a**nd **r**anging) is used to detect the speed and location of objects. **Figure 8** shows a police officer using radar to determine the speed of a car. The officer points the radar device at a car and presses a button. The device emits short pulses of microwaves that reflect off the car and return to the device. The rate at which the waves are reflected is used to calculate the speed of the car. Radar is also used to monitor the movement of airplanes and to help ship captains navigate at night or in foggy weather.

Figure 8 *Police officers use radar to detect cars going faster than the speed limit.*

Infrared Waves

Infrared waves have shorter wavelengths and higher frequencies than microwaves. So infrared waves can carry more energy than microwaves and radio waves carry.

When you sit outside on a sunny summer day, you feel warm because of *infrared waves* emitted by the sun. Infrared waves are absorbed by your skin when they strike your body. The energy of the waves causes the particles in your skin to vibrate faster, and you feel the increased vibration as an increase in temperature.

The sun is not the only source of infrared waves. Objects that emit infrared waves include stars, planets, buildings, trees, and you! The amount of infrared radiation emitted by an object varies depending on the object's temperature. Warmer objects give off more infrared radiation than cooler objects.

Your eyes can't see infrared waves, but there are devices that can detect infrared radiation. For example, infrared binoculars convert infrared radiation into light you can see. Such binoculars can be used to observe animals at night. **Figure 9** shows how certain photographic films are sensitive to infrared radiation.

Figure 9 *In this photograph, brighter colors indicate higher temperatures.*

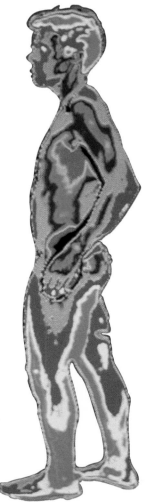

SECTION REVIEW

1. How do infrared waves differ from radio waves in terms of frequency and wavelength?

2. Describe two ways that radio waves are used for transmitting information.

3. **Inferring Relationships** Why do the frequencies of EM waves increase as the wavelengths decrease?

The Nature of Light **69**

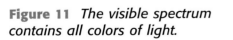
Visible Light

Visible light is the very narrow range of wavelengths and frequencies in the electromagnetic spectrum that humans can see. Humans see the different wavelengths as different colors, as shown in **Figure 10.** The longest wavelengths are seen as red light, and the shortest wavelengths are seen as violet light. Because violet light has the shortest wavelength, it carries the most energy of the visible light waves.

Figure 10 *White light, such as light from the sun, is actually visible light of all wavelengths combined. You see all the colors of visible light in a rainbow.*

Colors of Light The range of colors is called the *visible spectrum.* When you list the colors, you might use the imaginary name "Roy G. Biv" to help you remember their order. The letters in Roy's name represent the first letter of each color of visible light: **r**ed, **o**range, **y**ellow, **g**reen, **b**lue, **i**ndigo, and **v**iolet. When all the colors of visible light are combined, you see the light as white light. Sunlight and light from incandescent light bulbs and fluorescent light bulbs are examples of white light. You can see the visible spectrum in **Figure 11.**

Figure 11 *The visible spectrum contains all colors of light.*

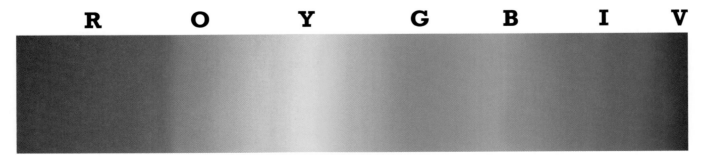

R O Y G B I V

Ultraviolet Light

Ultraviolet light is another type of electromagnetic wave produced by the sun. Ultraviolet waves have shorter wavelengths and higher frequencies than visible light. Therefore, ultraviolet waves carry more energy than visible light carries. This greater amount of energy affects us in both positive and negative ways.

Positive Effects On the positive side, ultraviolet waves produced artificially by ultraviolet lamps are used to kill bacteria on food and surgical instruments. In addition, limited exposure to ultraviolet light is beneficial to your body. When exposed to ultraviolet light, skin cells produce vitamin D, a substance necessary for the absorption of calcium by the intestines. Without calcium, your teeth and bones would be very weak.

Negative Effects On the negative side, overexposure to ultraviolet light can cause sunburn, skin cancer, damage to the eyes, wrinkles, and premature aging of the skin. Fortunately, much of the ultraviolet light from the sun does not reach the surface of the Earth. But you should still protect yourself against the ultraviolet light that does reach you. To do so, you should use sunscreen with a high SPF (**S**un **P**rotection **F**actor) and wear sunglasses that block out ultraviolet light, like the person on the left in **Figure 12.** You need this protection even on overcast days because ultraviolet light can travel through clouds.

Figure 12 *Sunscreen offers protection against a painful sunburn.*

Blocking the Sun

Sunscreens contain a chemical that prevents ultraviolet light from penetrating your skin. When you look at a bottle of sunscreen, you will see the abbreviation SPF followed by a number. The number is a guide to how long you can stay in the sun without getting a sunburn. For example, if you use a sunscreen with SPF 15 and you normally burn after being in the sun for 10 minutes, you will be able to stay in the sun for 150 minutes without getting burned. Why do you think people who burn easily need a higher SPF?

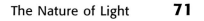

X Rays and Gamma Rays

X rays and gamma rays have some of the shortest wavelengths and highest frequencies of all EM waves. X rays carry a great deal of energy and easily penetrate a variety of materials. This characteristic makes X rays useful in the medical field, as shown in **Figure 13.** However, too much exposure to X rays can damage or kill living cells. Patients receiving X-ray examinations often wear a lead-lined apron to protect the parts of the body that do not need X-ray exposure.

Figure 13 *If you fall and hurt your arm, a doctor might use an X-ray machine to check for broken bones.*

 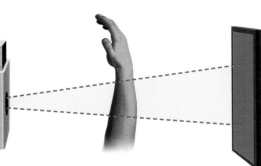 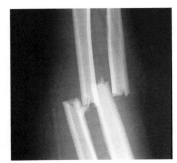

X rays travel easily through skin and muscle but are absorbed by bones.

The X rays that are not absorbed strike the film.

Bright areas appear on the film where X rays are absorbed by the bones.

Gamma rays carry large amounts of energy and can penetrate materials very easily. Every day you are exposed to small amounts of gamma rays that do not harm you. Because of their high energy, gamma rays are used to treat some forms of cancer. Radiologists focus the rays on tumors inside the body to kill the cancer cells. While this treatment can have positive effects, it often has negative side effects because some healthy cells are also killed.

internetconnect

SC*i*LINKS
NSTA

TOPIC: The Electromagnetic Spectrum
GO TO: www.scilinks.org
*sci*LINKS NUMBER: HSTP530

SECTION REVIEW

1. Explain why ultraviolet light, X rays, and gamma rays can be both helpful and harmful.

2. Describe how three different types of electromagnetic waves have been useful to you today.

3. **Comparing Concepts** Compare the wavelengths and frequencies of infrared, ultraviolet, and visible light. How does the energy carried by each type of wave compare with the others?

What You'll Do

- ◆ Compare regular reflection with diffuse reflection.
- ◆ Describe absorption and scattering of light.
- ◆ Explain how refraction can create optical illusions and separate white light into colors.
- ◆ Describe diffraction and interference of light.

Interactions of Light Waves

Have you ever seen a cat's eyes glow in the dark when light shines on them? Cats have a special layer of cells in the back of their eyes that reflects light. This layer helps the cat see better by giving the eyes another chance to detect the light. Reflection is just one way light waves interact. All types of EM waves interact in several ways. Because we can see visible light, it is easier to explain interactions involving visible light.

Reflection

Reflection occurs when light or any other wave bounces off an object. When you see yourself in a mirror, you are actually seeing light that has been reflected twice—first from you and then from the mirror. Reflection allows you to see objects that don't produce their own light. When light strikes an object, some of the light reflects off of it and is detected by your eyes.

But if light is reflecting off you and off the objects around you, why can't you see your reflection on a wall? To answer this question, you must first learn about the law of reflection.

The Law of Reflection Light reflects off surfaces the same way that a ball bounces off the ground. If you throw the ball straight down against a smooth surface, it will bounce straight up. If you bounce it at an angle, it will bounce away at an angle. The **law of reflection** states that the angle of incidence is equal to the angle of reflection. *Incidence* is the falling of a beam of light on a surface. **Figure 14** illustrates this law.

Figure 14 The Law of Reflection

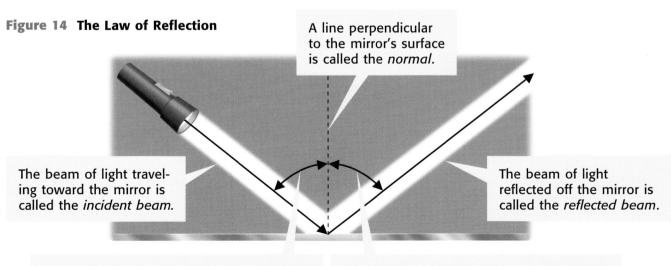

A line perpendicular to the mirror's surface is called the *normal*.

The beam of light traveling toward the mirror is called the *incident beam*.

The beam of light reflected off the mirror is called the *reflected beam*.

The angle between the incident beam and the normal is called the *angle of incidence*.

The angle between the reflected beam and the normal is called the *angle of reflection*.

Types of Reflection So back to the question, "Why can you see your reflection in a mirror but not in a wall?" The answer has to do with the differences between the two surfaces. If the reflecting surface is very smooth, like a mirror or polished metal, light beams reflect off all points of the surface at the same angle. This is called *regular reflection*. If the reflecting surface is slightly rough, like a wall, light beams will hit the surface and reflect at many different angles. This is called *diffuse reflection*. **Figure 15** illustrates the difference between the two types of reflection.

Figure 15 Regular Reflection Vs. Diffuse Reflection

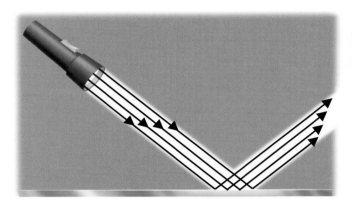

Regular reflection occurs when light beams are reflected at the same angle. When your eye detects the reflected beams, you can see a reflection on the surface.

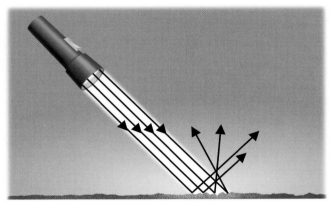

Diffuse reflection occurs when light beams reflect at many different angles. You can't see a reflection because not all of the reflected light is directed toward your eyes.

Figure 16 *A beam of light becomes dimmer partially because of absorption and scattering.*

Absorption and Scattering

You have probably noticed that when you use a flashlight, objects that are closer to you appear brighter than objects that are farther away. The light appears to weaken the farther it travels from the flashlight. This happens partially because the beam spreads out and partially because of absorption and scattering.

Absorption of Light The transfer of energy carried by light waves to particles of matter is called **absorption.** When you shine a flashlight in the air, the air particles absorb some of the energy from the light. This causes the light to become dim, as shown in **Figure 16.** The farther the light travels from the flashlight, the more it is absorbed by air particles.

Scattering of Light The release of light energy by particles of matter that have absorbed energy is called **scattering.** When the light is released, it scatters in all directions. Light from a flashlight is scattered out of the beam by air particles. This scattered light allows you to see objects outside of the beam, as shown in Figure 16 on the previous page. However, because light is scattered out of the beam, the beam becomes dimmer.

Scattering makes the sky blue. Light with shorter wavelengths is scattered more than light with longer wavelengths. Sunlight is made up of many different colors of light, but blue light (which has a very short wavelength) is scattered more than any other color. So when you look at the sky, you see a background of blue light. You can learn more about the scattering of light by doing the QuickLab at right.

Refraction

Imagine that you and a friend are at a lake. Your friend wades into the water. You look at her and are startled to see that her feet look like they are separated from her legs! You know her feet did not come off, so how can you explain what you see? The answer has to do with refraction.

Refraction is the bending of a wave as it passes at an angle from one medium to another. Refraction of light waves occurs because the speed of light varies depending on the material through which the waves are traveling. In a vacuum, light travels at 300,000,000 m/s, but it travels more slowly through matter. When a wave enters a new medium at an angle, the part of the wave that enters first begins traveling at a different speed from the rest of the wave. **Figure 17** shows how a light beam is bent by refraction.

⏰ uick Lab

Scattering Milk

1. Fill a clear **2 L plastic bottle** with **water.**

2. Turn the lights off, and shine a **flashlight** through the water. Look at the water from all sides of the bottle. Describe what you see in your ScienceLog.

3. Add a few drops of **milk** to the water, and shake the bottle to mix it up.

4. Repeat step 2. Describe any color changes. If you don't see any, add more milk until you do.

5. How is the water-and-milk mixture like air particles in the atmosphere? Write your answer in your ScienceLog.

TRY at HOME

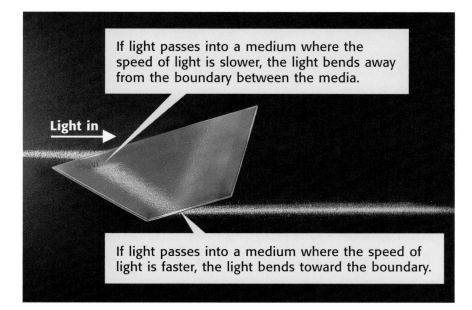

Figure 17 *Light travels more slowly through glass than it does through air. Therefore, light refracts as it passes at an angle from air to glass or from glass to air.*

If light passes into a medium where the speed of light is slower, the light bends away from the boundary between the media.

Light in →

If light passes into a medium where the speed of light is faster, the light bends toward the boundary.

Optical Illusions Normally when you look at an object, the light reflecting off the object travels in a straight line from the object to your eye. Your brain always interprets light as traveling in straight lines. However, when you look at an object that is underwater, the light reflecting off the object does *not* travel in a straight line. Instead, it refracts. **Figure 18** shows how refraction creates an optical illusion.

Figure 18 *Refraction can create the illusion that the feet of the person in the water are separated from her legs. Try this for yourself!*

Refraction and Color Separation You have already learned that white light is actually composed of all the colors of visible light. You also know that the different colors correspond to different wavelengths. When white light is refracted, the amount that the light bends depends on its wavelength. Light waves with short wavelengths bend more than light waves with long wavelengths. Because of this, white light can be separated into different colors during refraction, as shown in **Figure 19.** Color separation during refraction is responsible for the formation of rainbows. Rainbows are created when sunlight is refracted by water droplets.

Figure 19 *A prism is a piece of glass that separates white light into the colors of visible light by refraction.*

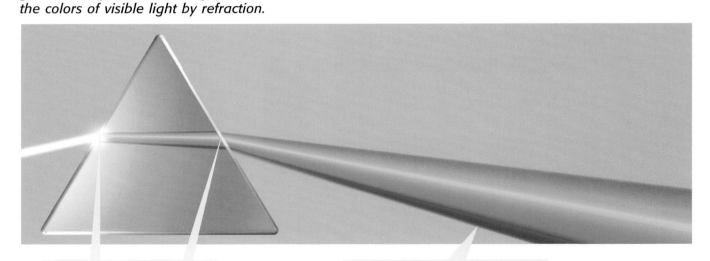

Light passing through a prism is refracted twice— once when it enters and once when it exits.

Violet light, which has a short wavelength, is refracted more than red light, which has a long wavelength.

Diffraction

Refraction isn't the only way light waves are bent. **Diffraction** is the bending of waves around barriers or through openings. The diffraction of light waves is not always easy to see. The diffraction of water waves, shown in **Figure 20,** is easier to see. The amount a wave diffracts depends on its wavelength and the size of the barrier or the opening. The greatest amount of diffraction occurs when the barrier or opening is the same size or smaller than the wavelength.

The wavelength of light is very small—about 100 times smaller than the thickness of a human hair! So in order for light to diffract very much, light has to be passing through a slit or some other opening that is very narrow.

Light waves cannot diffract very much around large obstacles, such as buildings. That's why you can't see around corners. But light waves always diffract a small amount. You can observe light waves diffracting if you examine the edges of a shadow. Diffraction causes the edges of shadows to be blurry.

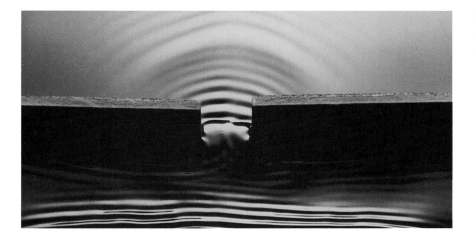

Figure 20 *Water waves are often used to model the behavior of light waves.*

Interference

Interference is a wave interaction that occurs when two or more waves overlap. Overlapping waves can combine by constructive or destructive interference.

Constructive Interference When waves combine by *constructive interference,* the resulting wave has a greater amplitude than the individual waves had. Constructive interference of light waves can be observed when light of one wavelength shines through two small slits onto a screen. The light on the screen will appear as a series of alternating bright and dark bands. The bright bands result from light waves combining through constructive interference to create a light wave with a greater amplitude.

Two lamps are brighter than one, but it's not because of constructive interference. It's because two lamps produce more energy in the form of photons than one lamp. As a result, the light has a greater intensity, which makes the room brighter.

Destructive Interference When waves combine by *destructive interference,* the resulting wave has a smaller amplitude than the individual waves had. Therefore, when light waves interfere destructively, the result will be dimmer light.

You do not see constructive or destructive interference of white light. To understand why, remember that white light is composed of waves with many different wavelengths. The waves rarely line up to combine in total destructive interference. However, if light of only one wavelength is used, both constructive and destructive interference are easily observed, as illustrated in **Figure 21.**

Figure 21 **Constructive and Destructive Interference**

Red light of one wavelength passes between two tiny slits.

The light waves diffract as they pass through the tiny slits.

If you put a screen in front of the slits, you will see alternating bright and dark bands.

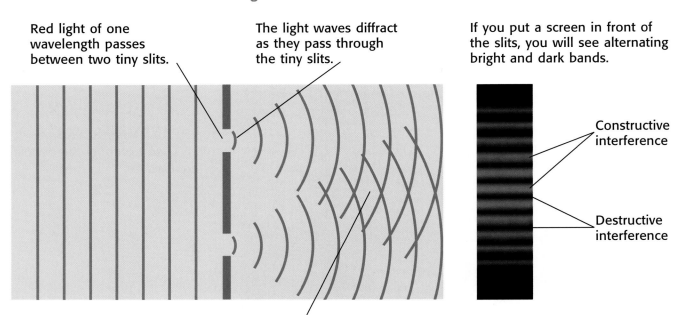

Constructive interference

Destructive interference

The diffracted light waves interfere both constructively and destructively.

internet**connect**

SCi**LINKS**
NSTA

TOPIC: Reflection and Refraction
GO TO: www.scilinks.org
*sci***LINKS NUMBER:** HSTP545

SECTION REVIEW

1. Explain the difference between absorption and scattering.

2. Why does a straw look bent in a glass of water?

3. Why do the edges of shadows seem blurry? Explain your answer.

4. **Applying Concepts** Explain why you can see your reflection on a spoon but not on a piece of cloth.

Light and Color

Terms to Learn

transmission   opaque
transparent   pigment
translucent

What You'll Do

◆ Name and describe the three ways light interacts with matter.
◆ Explain how the color of an object is determined.
◆ Compare the primary colors of light and the primary pigments.

Have you ever wondered what gives an object its color? You already know that white light is made of all the colors of light. But when you see fruit in white light, you see color. For example, strawberries are red and bananas are yellow. Why aren't they all white? And how can a soda bottle be green and let you see through it at the same time? To answer these questions, you must first learn how light interacts with matter. Then you will understand why objects have different colors.

Light and Matter

When light strikes any form of matter, it can interact with the matter in three different ways—it can be reflected, absorbed, or transmitted. You learned about reflection and absorption in the previous section. **Transmission** is the passing of light through matter. You see the transmission of light all the time. All of the light that reaches your eyes is transmitted through air. Light can interact with matter in several ways at the same time, as shown in **Figure 22.**

Figure 22 *Light is transmitted, reflected, and absorbed when it strikes the glass in a window.*

You can see the glass and your reflection in it because light is **reflected** off the glass.

You can see objects outside because light is **transmitted** through the glass.

The glass feels warm when you touch it because some light is **absorbed** by the glass.

Types of Matter Matter through which visible light is easily transmitted is said to be **transparent.** Air, glass, and water are examples of transparent matter. You can see objects clearly when you view them through transparent matter.

Sometimes windows in bathrooms are made of frosted glass. If you try to look through one of these types of windows, you will see only blurry shapes. You can't see clearly through a frosted window because it is translucent. **Translucent** matter transmits light but also scatters the light as it passes through the matter. Wax paper is an example of translucent matter.

Matter that does not transmit any light is said to be **opaque.** You cannot see through opaque objects. Metal, wood, and this book are examples of opaque objects. You can compare transparent, translucent, and opaque matter in **Figure 23.**

Figure 23 What's for Lunch?

Translucent wax paper makes it a little harder to see exactly what's for lunch.

Transparent plastic makes it easy to see what you are having for lunch.

Opaque aluminum foil makes it impossible to see your lunch without unwrapping it.

Colors of Objects

How does the interaction of light with matter determine an object's color? You already know that the color of light is determined by the wavelength of the light wave. Red has the longest wavelength, violet has the shortest wavelength, and other colors have wavelengths in between.

The color that an object appears to be is determined by the wavelengths of light that reach your eyes. Light reaches your eyes after being reflected off an object or after being transmitted through an object. After reaching your eyes, light is converted into electrical impulses and interpreted by your brain as colors.

What's a bean's favorite color? It's not a riddle, it's an experiment on page 132 of the LabBook.

Colors of Opaque Objects When white light strikes a colored opaque object, some colors of light are absorbed and some are reflected. Only the light that is reflected reaches your eyes and is detected. Therefore, the colors of light that are reflected by an opaque object determine the color you see. For example, if your sweater reflects blue light and absorbs all other colors, you will see that the sweater is blue. Another example is shown in **Figure 24.**

✓ Self-Check

If blue light shines on a white sheet of paper, what color does the paper appear to be?

(Turn to page 152 to check your answer.)

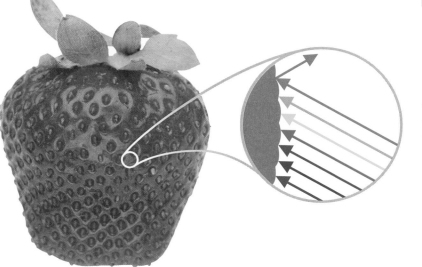

Figure 24 *When white light shines on a strawberry, only red light is reflected. All other colors of light are absorbed. Therefore, the strawberry looks red to you.*

If green objects reflect green light and red objects reflect red light, what colors of light are reflected by the cow shown at right? Remember that white light includes all colors of light. So white objects—such as the white hair in the cow's hide—appear white because all the colors of light are reflected. On the other hand, black is the absence of color. When light strikes a black object, all the colors are absorbed.

Colors of Transparent and Translucent Objects
The color of transparent and translucent objects is determined differently from the color of opaque objects. Ordinary window glass is colorless in white light because it transmits all the colors that strike it. However, some transparent objects are colored. When you look through colored transparent or translucent objects, you see the color of light that was transmitted through the material. All the other colors were absorbed, as shown in **Figure 25.**

Figure 25 *This bottle is green because the plastic transmits only green light.*

The Nature of Light   **81**

Rose-Colored Glasses?

1. Obtain **four plastic filters**—red, blue, yellow, and green.

2. Look through one filter at an object across the room. Describe the object's color.

3. Repeat step 2 with each of the filters.

4. Repeat step 2 with two or three filters together.

5. Why do you think the colors change when you use more than one filter?

6. Write your observations and answers in your ScienceLog.

Mixing Colors of Light

In order to get white light, you need to combine all colors of light, right? Well, that's one way of doing it. You can also get white light by adding just three colors of light together—red, blue, and green—as shown in **Figure 26.** In fact, these three colors can be combined in different ratios to produce all colors of visible light. Red, blue, and green are therefore called the *primary colors of light.*

Color Addition When colors of light combine, more wavelengths of light are present. Therefore, combining colors of light is called color addition. When two primary colors are added together, a *secondary color* is produced. The secondary colors are cyan (blue plus green), magenta (blue plus red), and yellow (red plus green).

Figure 26 *Primary colors—written in white—combine to produce white light. Secondary colors—written in black—are the result of two primary colors added together.*

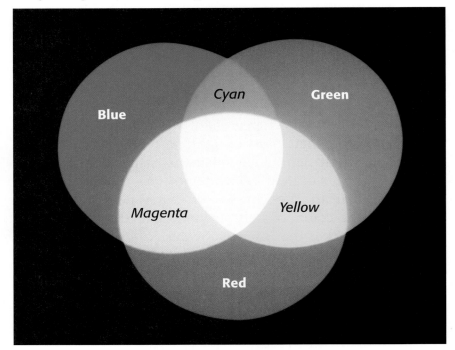

Mixing Colors of Pigment

If you have ever tried mixing paints in art class, you know that you can't make white paint by mixing red, blue, and green paint. The difference between mixing paint and mixing light is due to the fact that paint contains pigments. A **pigment** is a material that gives a substance its color by absorbing some colors of light and reflecting others.

Almost everything contains pigments. In fact, pigments give objects color. Chlorophyll and melanin are two examples of pigments. Chlorophyll gives plants a green color, and melanin gives your skin its color.

Color Subtraction Each pigment absorbs at least one color of light. When you mix pigments together, more colors of light are absorbed, or subtracted. Therefore, mixing colors of pigments is called color subtraction.

The *primary pigments* are yellow, cyan, and magenta. They can be combined to produce any other color. In fact, all the colors in this book were produced by using just the primary pigments and black ink. The black ink was used to provide contrast to the images. **Figure 27** shows how the four pigments combine to produce many different colors.

Geology
C O N N E C T I O N

Minerals are naturally occurring crystalline solids. A blue mineral called azurite was once used by European painters as a pigment in paint. But these painters didn't realize that azurite changes into another mineral over time. The new mineral, malachite, is green. So some paintings that once had beautiful blue skies now have skies that look greenish.

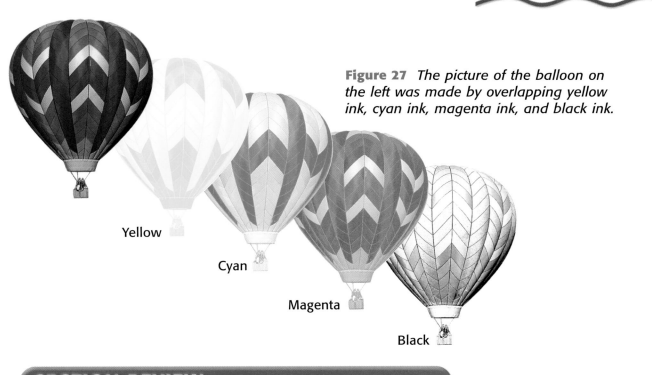

Figure 27 *The picture of the balloon on the left was made by overlapping yellow ink, cyan ink, magenta ink, and black ink.*

Yellow

Cyan

Magenta

Black

SECTION REVIEW

1. Describe three different ways light interacts with matter.

2. What are the primary colors of light, and why are they called primary colors?

3. Describe the difference between the primary colors of light and the primary pigments.

4. **Applying Concepts** Explain what happens to the different colors of light when white light shines on a violet object.

Mixing Colors

Mix two colors, such as red and green, and you create a new color. Is the new color brighter or darker? Color and brightness depend on the light that reaches your eye. And what reaches your eye depends on whether you are adding colors (combining wavelengths by mixing colors of light) or subtracting colors (absorbing wavelengths by mixing colors of pigments). In this activity, you will do both types of color formation and see the results firsthand!

MATERIALS

Part A
- 3 flashlights
- colored filters–red, green, and blue
- white paper
- masking tape

Part B
- 2 small plastic or paper cups
- water
- paintbrush
- watercolor paints
- masking tape
- white paper
- metric ruler

Part A: Color Addition

Procedure

1 Tape a colored filter over each flashlight lens.

2 In a darkened room, shine the red light on a sheet of clean white paper. Then shine the blue light next to the red light. You should have two circles of light, one red and one blue, next to each other.

3 Move the flashlights so that the circles overlap by about half their diameter. What color is formed in the area? Is the mixed area brighter or darker than the single-color areas? Record your observations.

4 Repeat steps 2 and 3 with the red and green lights.

5 Now shine all three lights at the same point on the paper. Record your observations.

Analysis

6 In general, when you mixed two colors, was the result brighter or darker than the original colors?

7 In step 5, you mixed all three colors. Was the resulting color brighter or darker than when you mixed two colors? Explain your answer in terms of color addition.

8 What do you think would happen if you mixed together all the colors of light? Explain your answer.

Part B: Color Subtraction

Procedure

9 Place a piece of masking tape on each cup. Label one cup "Clean" and the other cup "Dirty." Fill each cup about half full with water.

10 Wet the paintbrush thoroughly in the Clean cup. Using the watercolor paints, paint a red circle on the white paper. The circle should be approximately 4 cm in diameter.

11 Clean the brush by rinsing it first in the Dirty cup and then in the Clean cup.

12 Paint a blue circle next to the red circle. Then paint half the red circle with the blue paint.

13 Examine the three areas: red, blue, and mixed. What color is the mixed area? Does it appear brighter or darker than the red and blue areas? Record your observations in your ScienceLog.

14 Clean the brush. Paint a green circle 4 cm in diameter, and then paint half the blue circle with green paint.

15 Examine the green, blue, and mixed areas. Record your observations.

16 Now add green paint to the mixed red-blue area so that you have an area that is a mixture of red, green, and blue paint. Clean your brush.

17 Record your observations of this new mixed area.

Analysis

18 In general, when you mixed two colors, was the result brighter or darker than the original colors?

19 In step 16, you mixed all three colors. Was the result brighter or darker than the result from mixing two colors? Explain your answer in terms of color subtraction.

20 Based on your results, what do you think would happen if you mixed all the colors of paint? Explain your answer.

Chapter Highlights

SECTION 1

Vocabulary
electromagnetic wave *(p. 62)*
radiation *(p. 63)*

Section Notes

• Light is an electromagnetic (EM) wave. An electromagnetic wave is a wave that travels as vibrating electric and magnetic fields. EM waves require no medium through which to travel.

• Electromagnetic waves are produced by the vibration of electrically charged particles.

• The speed of light in a vacuum is 300,000,000 m/s.

SECTION 2

Vocabulary
electromagnetic spectrum *(p. 65)*

Section Notes

• All EM waves travel at the speed of light. EM waves differ only by wavelength and frequency.

• The entire range of EM waves is called the electromagnetic spectrum.

• Radio waves are most often used for communication.

• Microwaves are used for cooking and in radar.

• Infrared waves have shorter wavelengths and higher frequencies than microwaves. The absorption of infrared waves is felt as an increase in temperature.

• Visible light is the very narrow range of wavelengths that humans can see. Different wavelengths are seen as different colors.

• Ultraviolet light is useful for killing bacteria and for producing vitamin D in the body, but overexposure can cause health problems.

• X rays and gamma rays are EM waves that are often used in medicine. Overexposure to these EM waves can damage or kill living cells.

☑ Skills Check

Math Concepts

DISTANCE To calculate the distance that light travels in space, multiply the amount of time light travels by the speed of light in a vacuum. The speed of light in a vacuum is 300,000,000 m/s. If light from a star travels for 192 seconds before reaching a planet, then the distance the light traveled can be calculated as follows:

distance = speed of light × time

distance = 300,000,000 m/s × 192 s

distance = 57,600,000,000 m

Visual Understanding

THE PRODUCTION OF LIGHT Light is produced by the vibration of electrically charged particles. Repeated vibrations of these particles, or electrons, release tiny "packets" of energy called photons. Review Figure 2 on page 63 to see how light and other electromagnetic waves are the result of electron movement.

SECTION 3

Vocabulary

reflection *(p. 73)*
law of reflection *(p. 73)*
absorption *(p. 74)*
scattering *(p. 75)*
refraction *(p. 75)*
diffraction *(p. 77)*
interference *(p. 77)*

Section Notes

- Two types of reflection are regular and diffuse reflection.
- Absorption and scattering cause light beams to become dimmer with distance.
- How much a light beam bends during refraction depends on the light's wavelength.
- Light waves diffract more when traveling through a narrow opening.
- Interference of light waves can cause bright and dark bands.

SECTION 4

Vocabulary

transmission *(p. 79)*
transparent *(p. 80)*
translucent *(p. 80)*
opaque *(p. 80)*
pigment *(p. 82)*

Section Notes

- Objects are classified as transparent, translucent, or opaque depending on their ability to transmit light.
- Colors of opaque objects are determined by the color of light they reflect. White opaque objects reflect all colors and black opaque objects absorb all colors.
- Colors of transparent and translucent objects are determined by the color of light they transmit. All other colors are absorbed.

- White light is a mixture of all colors of light. The primary colors of light are red, blue, and green.
- Pigments give objects color. The primary pigments are magenta, cyan, and yellow.

Labs

What Color of Light Is Best for Green Plants? *(p. 132)*
Which Color Is Hottest? *(p. 133)*

---

internetconnect

GO TO: go.hrw.com

Visit the **HRW** Web site for a variety of learning tools related to this chapter. Just type in the keyword:

KEYWORD: HSTLGT

GO TO: www.scilinks.org

Visit the **National Science Teachers Association** on-line Web site for Internet resources related to this chapter. Just type in the *sci*LINKS number for more information about the topic:

TOPIC: Using Light	*sci*LINKS NUMBER: HSTP528
TOPIC: Light Energy	*sci*LINKS NUMBER: HSTP529
TOPIC: The Electromagnetic Spectrum	*sci*LINKS NUMBER: HSTP530
TOPIC: Reflection and Refraction	*sci*LINKS NUMBER: HSTP545
TOPIC: Colors	*sci*LINKS NUMBER: HSTP550

Chapter Review

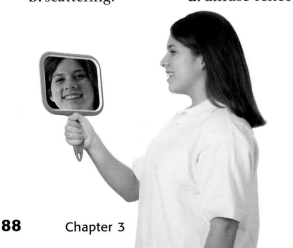

Concept Mapping

18. Use the following terms to create a concept map: light, matter, reflection, absorption, scattering, transmission.

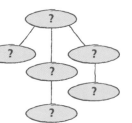

CRITICAL THINKING AND PROBLEM SOLVING

19. A tern is a type of bird that dives underwater to catch fish. When a young tern begins learning to catch fish, it is rarely successful. The tern has to learn that when a fish appears to be in a certain place underwater, the fish is actually in a slightly different place. Explain why the tern sees the fish in the wrong place.

20. Radio waves and gamma rays are both types of electromagnetic waves. Exposure to radio waves does not harm the human body, whereas exposure to gamma rays can be extremely dangerous. What is the difference between these types of EM waves? Why are gamma rays more dangerous?

21. If you look around a parking lot during the summer, you might notice sun shades set up in the windshields of cars. Explain how the sun shades help keep the inside of a car cool.

MATH IN SCIENCE

22. Calculate the time it takes for light from the sun to reach Mercury. Mercury is 54,900,000,000 m away from the sun.

INTERPRETING GRAPHICS

23. Each of the pictures below shows the effects of a wave interaction of light. Identify the interaction involved.

Reading Check-up Take a minute to review your answers to the Pre-Reading Questions found at the bottom of page 60. Have your answers changed? If necessary, revise your answers based on what you have learned since you began this chapter.

Science, Technology, and Society

Fireflies Light the Way

Just as beams of light from coastal light-houses warn boats of approaching danger, scientists are using the light of an unlikely source—fireflies—to warn food inspectors of life-threatening bacterial contamination! Thousands of people die each year from meat contaminated with bacteria. The light from fireflies is being used to study several diseases, waste-water treatment, and environmental protection as well!

Nature's Guiding Light

A number of organisms, including some fishes, squids, beetles, and bacteria, emit light. Fireflies, in particular, use this light to attract mates. How do these organisms use energy to emit light?

Remarkably, all of these organisms use one enzyme to make light, an enzyme called *luciferase*. This enzyme breaks down *adenosine triphosphate* (ATP) to create energy. This energy is used to excite electrons to produce light in the form of a glow or flash. Fireflies are very effective light bulbs. Nearly 100 percent of the energy they get from ATP is given off as light. Only 10 percent of energy given off by electrical light bulbs is in the form of light; the other 90 percent is thermal energy!

Harnessing Life's Light

How have scientists harnessed the firefly's ability to produce light to find bacteria? Researchers have found the gene responsible for making luciferase. Scientists have taken the gene from fireflies that makes luciferase and inserted it into a virus that preys on bacteria. The virus isn't harmful to humans and can be mixed into meat to help scientists detect bacteria. When the virus infects the bacteria, it transfers the gene into the genetic machinery of the bacteria. This bacteria then produces luciferase and glows!

▲ *The firefly* (Photuris pyralis) *is helping food inspectors save thousands of lives each year!*

This process is being used to find a number of dangerous bacteria that contaminate foods, including *Salmonella* and *Escherichia coli.* These bacteria are responsible for thousands of deaths each year. Not only is the test effective, it is fast. Before researchers developed this test, it took up to 3 days to determine whether food was contaminated by bacteria. By that time, the food was already at the grocery store!

Think About It!

▶ What color of light would you hypothesize gives plants the most energy? Investigate, and see if your hypothesis is right!

90

Eureka!

It's a Heat Wave!

Percy L. Spencer never stopped looking for answers. In fact, he patented 120 inventions in his 39 years with the company Raytheon. During a routine visit to one of the Raytheon laboratories in 1946, Spencer found that a candy bar had melted inside his coat pocket. He could have just chalked this up to body heat, but he didn't. Instead, he took a closer look at his surroundings and noticed a nearby magnetron—a tube he designed to produce microwaves for radar systems.

A Popping Test

This made Spencer curious. Did the microwaves from the magnetron melt the candy bar, and if so, could microwaves be used to heat other things? Spencer answered his questions by putting a bag of unpopped corn kernels next to a magnetron. The kernels popped! Spencer had just made the first "microwave" popcorn! The test was a huge success. This simple experiment showed that a magnetron could heat foods with microwaves, and it could heat them quickly. When Spencer patented his invention in 1953, he called it a "High Frequency Dielectric Heating Apparatus."

Perfect Timing!

Spencer originally designed magnetrons for radar machines used in World War II. Discovering another use for them was well timed. After the war, the military had little use for the 10,000 magnetrons a week that Raytheon could manufacture. So Raytheon decided to use the magnetrons to power Spencer's "High Frequency Dielectric

The first microwave oven, known as a "Radarange," 1953 ▲

Heating Apparatus." But first the company had to come up with a simpler name! The winning entry in the renaming contest was "Radar Range," which later became one word, *Radarange*.

An Inconvenient Convenience

The first Radaranges had a few drawbacks. For one thing, they were very expensive. They also weighed over 340 kg and were 1.6 m tall. Try fitting that on your kitchen counter! Because the Radarange was so large and expensive, only restaurants, railroad companies, and cruise ships used them. By 1967, improvements in the design made the Radarange compact and affordable, similar to the microwave ovens of today.

Now You're Cooking!

Just how do microwave ovens cook food? It just so happens that microwaves are absorbed by water molecules in the food being cooked. When water molecules throughout the food absorb microwaves, they start to move faster. As a result, the food's temperature increases. Leftovers anyone?

Find Out for Yourself

▶ Microwaves make water molecules in food move faster. This is what increases the temperature of food that is cooked in a microwave. But did you know that most dishes will not heat up in a microwave oven if there is no food on them? To discover why, find out what most dishes are made of. Then infer why empty dishes do not heat up in a microwave.

Light in Our World

Pre-Reading Questions

1. Name three sources of light.
2. How do mirrors and lenses form images?
3. How does the human eye detect light?

Bright Lights, Neon Lights

Look at the multicolored arcs of light in this photo. These "neon" lights are made by passing electricity through tubes filled with certain gases. Neon, argon, krypton, helium, and mercury gases each light up as a different dazzling color. In this chapter, you will learn how different kinds of light are produced and how images that reflect or focus light are formed. You will also learn how mirrors, lenses, and high-tech instruments focus or transmit light energy.

MIRROR, MIRROR

In this activity, you will explore images formed by plane mirrors.

Procedure

1. **Tape** a sheet of **graph paper** on your desk. Stand a **plane mirror** straight up in the middle of the paper. Hold the mirror in place with small pieces of **modeling clay.**

2. Count four grid squares from the mirror, and place a **pencil** there. Look in the mirror. How many squares behind the mirror is the image of the pencil? Move the pencil farther away from the mirror. How did the image change?

3. Replace the mirror with **colored glass.** Look at the pencil image in the glass. Compare it with the image you saw in the mirror.

4. Use a pencil to draw a square on the graph paper in front of the glass. Looking through the glass, trace the image of the square on the paper behind the glass. Using a **metric ruler,** measure and compare the sizes of the two squares.

Analysis

5. How does the distance from an object to a plane mirror compare with the apparent distance from the mirror to the object's image behind the mirror?

6. In general, how does the size of an object compare with that of its image in a plane mirror?

Terms to Learn

luminous   neon light
illuminated   vapor light
incandescent light
fluorescent light

What You'll Do

◆ Compare luminous and
  illuminated objects.
◆ Name four ways light can be
  produced.

Astronomy

C O N N E C T I O N

Sometimes the moon shines so
brightly that you might think there is
a lot of "moonlight." But did you
know that moonlight is actually sunlight? The moon does not give off
light. You can see the moon because
it is illuminated by light from the
sun. You see different phases of the
moon because light from the sun
shines only on the part of the moon
that faces the sun.

Light Sources

Although visible light represents only a small portion of the
electromagnetic spectrum, it has a huge effect on your life.
Visible light from the sun gives plants the energy necessary
for growth and reproduction. Without plants at the base of
the food chain, few other life-forms could exist. And of course,
without visible light, you could not see anything. Your eyes
are totally useless without sources of visible light.

Light Source or Reflection?

If you look at a television in a bright room, you see the cabinet around the television as well as the image on the screen.
But if you look at the same television in the dark, only the
image on the screen shows up. The difference is that the screen
is a light source, while the cabinet around the television isn't.

You can see a light source even in the dark because its light
passes directly into your eyes. Flames, light bulbs, fireflies, and
the sun are all light sources. Scientists describe objects that produce visible light as being **luminous** (LOO muh nuhs). **Figure 1**
shows examples of luminous objects.

Most of the objects around you are not light sources. But
you can still see them because light from a light source reflects
off the objects and then travels to your eyes. Scientists describe
a visible object that is not a light source as being **illuminated**
(i LOO muh NAYT ed).

Figure 1 *Television screens,
fires, and fireflies are luminous
objects.*

Producing Light

Light sources produce light in many ways. For example, if you heat a piece of metal enough, it will visibly glow red hot. Light can also be produced chemically, like the light produced by a firefly. Light can even be produced by sending an electric current through certain gases.

Incandescent Light If you have ever looked inside a toaster while toasting a piece of bread, you may have seen thin wires or bars glowing red. The wires give off energy as light when heated to a high temperature. Light produced by hot objects is called **incandescent** (IN kuhn DES uhnt) **light.** **Figure 2** shows a source of incandescent light that you have in your home.

Sources of incandescent light also release a large amount of thermal energy. Sometimes this thermal energy is useful because it can be used to cook food or to warm a room. But often this thermal energy is not used for anything. For example, the thermal energy given off by a light bulb is not very useful.

Halogen lights are another type of incandescent light. They were originally developed for use on the wings of airplanes, but they are now used in homes and in car headlights. **Figure 3** shows how halogen lights work.

Figure 2 *Light bulbs produce incandescent light.*

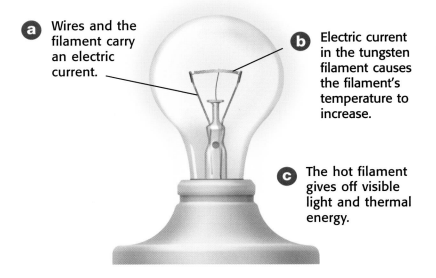

a Wires and the filament carry an electric current.

b Electric current in the tungsten filament causes the filament's temperature to increase.

c The hot filament gives off visible light and thermal energy.

Figure 3 *The way in which the tungsten from the filament can be used over and over again prevents the bulb from burning out too quickly.*

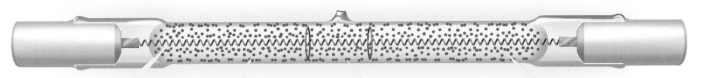

A tungsten filament, heated to about 3,000°C, glows very brightly and vaporizes.

The tungsten vapor (red particles) travels to the glass wall, where it cools to about 800°C.

At the lower temperature, tungsten combines with a halogen gas (blue particles) to form a new compound.

The new compound travels back to the filament, where it breaks down because of the high temperature. Tungsten from the compound is deposited on the filament and can be used again.

Fluorescent Light The light that comes from the long, cylindrical bulbs in your classroom is called fluorescent light. **Fluorescent** (FLOO uh RES uhnt) **light** is visible light emitted by a phosphor particle when it absorbs energy such as ultraviolet light. Fluorescent light is sometimes called cool light because less thermal energy is produced than with incandescent light. **Figure 4** shows how a fluorescent light bulb works.

Figure 4 Fluorescent Light

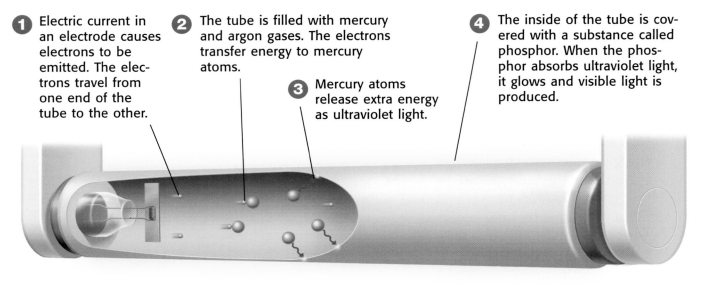

1 Electric current in an electrode causes electrons to be emitted. The electrons travel from one end of the tube to the other.

2 The tube is filled with mercury and argon gases. The electrons transfer energy to mercury atoms.

3 Mercury atoms release extra energy as ultraviolet light.

4 The inside of the tube is covered with a substance called phosphor. When the phosphor absorbs ultraviolet light, it glows and visible light is produced.

Neon Light The visible light emitted by atoms of certain gases, such as neon, when they absorb and then release energy is called **neon light**. **Figure 5** shows how neon light is produced.

A true neon light—one in which the tube is filled with neon gas—glows red. Other colors are produced when the tubes are filled with different gases. For example, sodium gas produces yellow light, and krypton gas produces purple light. A mixture of argon gas and mercury gas produces blue light.

Figure 5 Neon Light

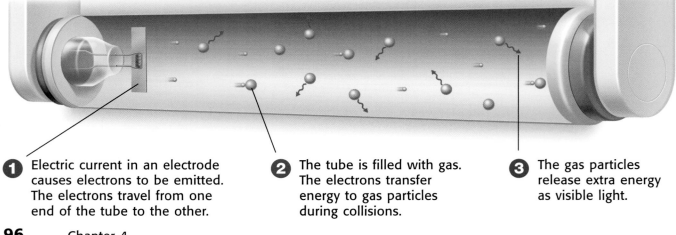

1 Electric current in an electrode causes electrons to be emitted. The electrons travel from one end of the tube to the other.

2 The tube is filled with gas. The electrons transfer energy to gas particles during collisions.

3 The gas particles release extra energy as visible light.

Vapor Light Another type of incandescent light, called **vapor light,** is produced when electrons combine with gaseous metal atoms. Street lamps usually contain either mercury vapor or sodium vapor. You can tell the difference by the color of the light. If the light is bluish, the lamp contains mercury vapor. If the light is orange, the lamp contains sodium vapor. Both kinds of vapor lamps produce light in similar ways, as described in **Figure 6.**

Stop! and go read about the invention of traffic lights on page 120.

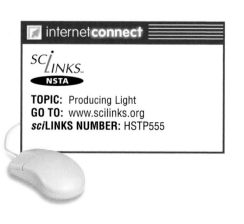

Figure 6 *Sodium vapor lights are very bright and do not produce much glare.*

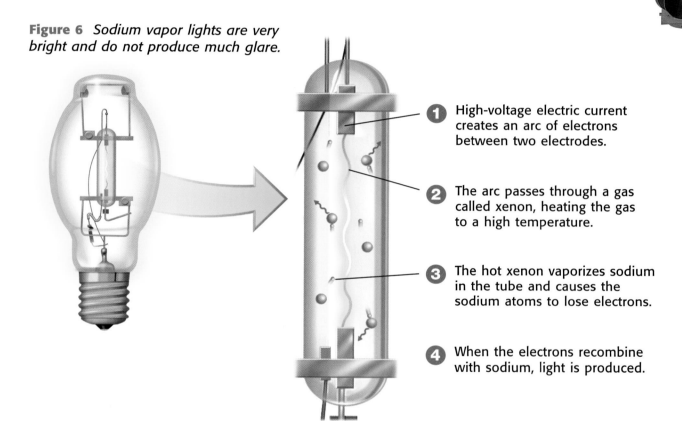

1 High-voltage electric current creates an arc of electrons between two electrodes.

2 The arc passes through a gas called xenon, heating the gas to a high temperature.

3 The hot xenon vaporizes sodium in the tube and causes the sodium atoms to lose electrons.

4 When the electrons recombine with sodium, light is produced.

SECTION REVIEW

1. Identify five illuminated objects in your classroom, and name the luminous object (or objects) providing the light.

2. Describe places where you might use incandescent light, fluorescent light, neon light, and vapor light.

3. Describe how fluorescent light is similar to neon light.

4. **Applying Concepts** Halogen bulbs emit bright light from small bulbs. They also emit thermal energy. Would you use a halogen bulb to study by? Why or why not?

internetconnect

SC*L*INKS
NSTA

TOPIC: Producing Light
GO TO: www.scilinks.org
*sci***LINKS NUMBER:** HSTP555

Terms to Learn

plane mirror   lens
concave mirror   convex lens
focal point   concave lens
convex mirror

What You'll Do

◆ Illustrate how mirrors and lenses form images using ray diagrams.
◆ Explain the difference between real and virtual images.
◆ Compare plane mirrors, concave mirrors, and convex mirrors.
◆ Explain how concave and convex lenses form images.

Mirrors and Lenses

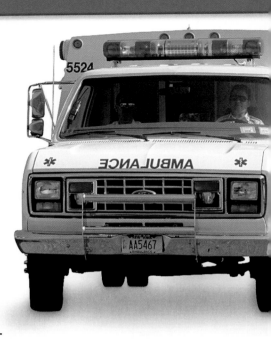

Look at the letters on the front of the ambulance shown at right. Do you notice anything strange about them? Some of the letters are backward, and they don't seem to spell a word.

The letters spell the word AMBULANCE when viewed in a mirror. Images in mirrors are reversed left to right. The word *ambulance* is spelled backward so that people driving cars can read it when they see the ambulance in their rearview mirror. To understand how images are formed in mirrors, you must first learn how to use rays to trace the path of light waves.

Rays Show the Path of Light Waves

Light is an electromagnetic wave. Light waves travel from their source in all directions. If you could trace the path of one wave as it travels away from a light source, you would find that the path is a straight line. Because light waves travel in straight lines, you can use an arrow called a *ray* to show the path and the direction of a light wave. **Figure 7** shows some rays coming from a light bulb.

Rays can also be used to show the path of light waves after the waves have been reflected or refracted. Therefore, rays in ray diagrams are often used to show changes in the direction light travels after being reflected by mirrors or refracted by lenses. You'll learn more about ray diagrams a little later in this section.

Figure 7 *Rays from this light bulb show the path and direction of some light waves produced by the bulb.*

Mirrors Reflect Light

Have you ever looked at your reflection in a metal spoon? The polished metal of the spoon acts like a mirror, but not like the mirror in your bathroom! If you look on one side of the spoon, your face is upside down. But if you look on the other side, your face is right side up. Why?

The shape of a reflecting surface affects the way light reflects from it. Therefore, the image you see in your bathroom mirror differs from the image you see in a spoon. Mirrors are classified by their shape. The different shapes are called plane, concave, and convex.

Plane Mirrors Most mirrors, such as the one in your bathroom, are plane mirrors. A **plane mirror** is a mirror with a flat surface. When you look in a plane mirror, your reflection is upright and is the same size as you are. Images in plane mirrors are reversed left to right, as shown in **Figure 8.**

When you look in a plane mirror, your image appears to be the same distance behind the mirror as you are in front of it. Why does your image seem to be behind the mirror? Because mirrors are opaque objects, light does not travel through them. But when light reflects off the mirror, your brain interprets the reflected light as if it travels in a straight line from behind the mirror. A *virtual image* is an image through which light does not actually travel. The image formed by a plane mirror is a virtual image. The ray diagram in **Figure 9** explains how light travels when you look into a mirror.

Figure 8 *Rearview mirrors in cars are plane mirrors.*

Figure 9 *The rays show how light reaches your eyes. The dotted lines show where the light appears to come from.*

Light reflects off of you and strikes the mirror, where it is reflected again. Some of the light reflecting off the mirror enters your eyes.

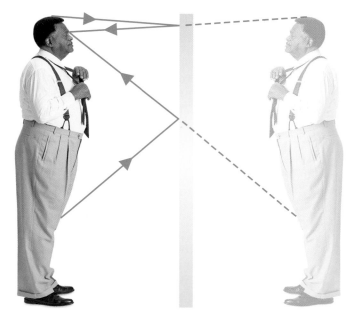

Your image appears to be behind the mirror because your brain assumes that the light rays that enter your eyes travel in a straight line from an object to your eyes.

Concave Mirrors Mirrors that are curved inward, such as the inside of a spoon, are called **concave mirrors.** Because the surfaces of concave mirrors are curved, the images formed by concave mirrors differ from the images formed by plane mirrors. To understand how concave mirrors form images, you must learn the terms illustrated in **Figure 10.**

Figure 10 *The image formed by a concave mirror depends on its optical axis, its focal point, and its focal length.*

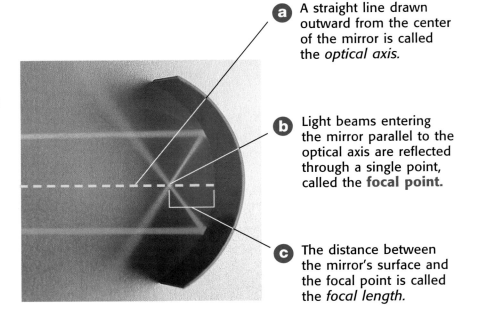

a A straight line drawn outward from the center of the mirror is called the *optical axis.*

b Light beams entering the mirror parallel to the optical axis are reflected through a single point, called the **focal point.**

c The distance between the mirror's surface and the focal point is called the *focal length.*

You already learned that plane mirrors can form only virtual images. Concave mirrors also form virtual images, but they can form *real images* too. A real image is an image through which light actually passes. A real image can be projected onto a screen; a virtual image cannot. To find out what kind of image a concave mirror forms, you can create a ray diagram. Just remember the following three rules when drawing ray diagrams for concave mirrors:

1 Draw a ray from the top of the object parallel to the optical axis. This ray will reflect through the focal point.

2 If the object is more than one focal length away from the mirror, draw a ray from the top of the object through the focal point. This ray will reflect parallel to the optical axis.

3 If the object is less than one focal length away from the mirror, draw a ray through the top of the object as if it came from the focal point. This ray will reflect parallel to the optical axis.

Real or Virtual For each ray diagram, you need to draw only two rays from the top of the object to find what kind of image is formed. If the reflected rays cross in front of the mirror, a real image is formed. The point where the rays cross is the top of the image. If the reflected rays do not cross, trace the reflected rays in straight lines behind the mirror. Those lines will cross to show where a virtual image is formed. Study **Figure 11** to better understand ray diagrams.

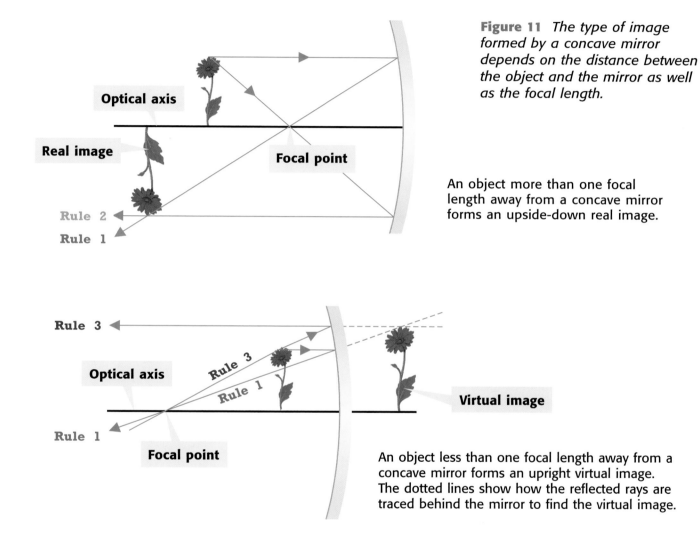

Figure 11 *The type of image formed by a concave mirror depends on the distance between the object and the mirror as well as the focal length.*

An object more than one focal length away from a concave mirror forms an upside-down real image.

An object less than one focal length away from a concave mirror forms an upright virtual image. The dotted lines show how the reflected rays are traced behind the mirror to find the virtual image.

Neither Real Nor Virtual If an object is placed at the focal point of a concave mirror, no image will form. Rule 2 explains why this happens—all rays that pass through the focal point on their way to the mirror will reflect parallel to the optical axis. Because all the reflected rays are parallel, they will never cross in front of or behind the mirror. If you place a light source at the focal point of a concave mirror, the light will reflect outward in a powerful light beam. Therefore, concave mirrors are used in car headlights and flashlights.

Convex Mirrors If you look at your reflection in the back of a spoon, you will notice that your image is right side up and small. The back of a spoon is a **convex mirror**—a mirror that curves out toward you. **Figure 12** shows how an image is formed by a convex mirror. All images formed by convex mirrors are virtual, upright, and smaller than the original object. Convex mirrors are useful because they produce images of a large area. This is the reason convex mirrors are often used for security in stores and factories. Convex mirrors are also used as side mirrors in cars and trucks.

Figure 12 *All images formed by convex mirrors are formed behind the mirror. Therefore, all images formed by convex mirrors are virtual.*

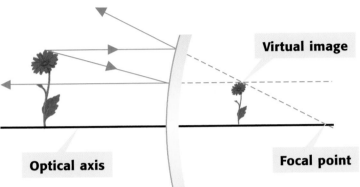

Virtual image

Optical axis

Focal point

APPLY

Convex Mirrors Help Drivers

The passenger side mirrors of most cars and trucks are convex mirrors. Convex mirrors are used because they help the driver see more of the traffic around the car than a plane mirror would. However, these mirrors are often stamped with the words "Objects in Mirror Are Closer Than They Appear." What property of convex mirrors makes this warning necessary? Why do you think the warning is important for drivers?

internet**connect**

SC*L*INKS.
NSTA

TOPIC: Mirrors
GO TO: www.scilinks.org
*sci*LINKS NUMBER: HSTP560

SECTION REVIEW

1. How is a concave mirror different from a convex mirror?

2. Draw a ray diagram showing how a concave mirror forms a real image.

3. **Applying Concepts** Plane mirrors, concave mirrors, and convex mirrors are useful at different times. Describe a situation in which you would use each type of mirror.

Lenses Refract Light

What do cameras, binoculars, telescopes, and movie projectors have in common? They all use lenses to create images. A **lens** is a curved, transparent object that forms an image by refracting, or bending, light. Like mirrors, lenses are classified by their shape. There are two types of lenses—convex and concave.

Convex Lenses A **convex lens** is thicker in the middle than at the edges. When light rays enter a convex lens, they refract toward the center. Light rays that enter a convex lens parallel to the optical axis are refracted so that they go through a focal point. The amount of refraction and the focal length depend on the curvature of the lens, as shown in **Figure 13.** Light rays that pass through the center of a lens are not refracted.

Convex lenses form many different kinds of images, depending on the focal length of the lens and the position of the object. For example, whenever you use a magnifying glass, you are using a convex lens to form an enlarged, virtual image. **Figure 14** illustrates how a magnifying lens works.

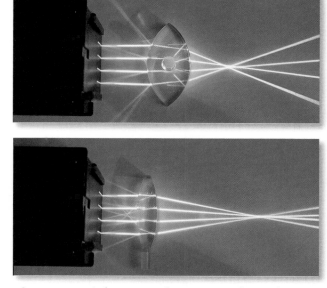

Figure 13 *Light rays refract more through convex lenses with greater curvature than through convex lenses with less curvature.*

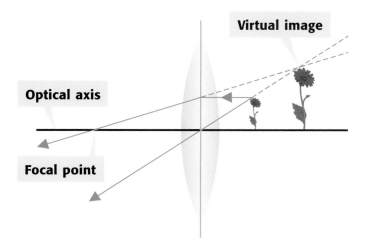

Figure 14 *If an object is less than one focal length away from a convex lens, a virtual image is formed. The image is larger than the object and can be seen only by looking into the lens.*

Convex lenses can also form real images. Movie projectors use convex lenses to focus real images on a screen. Cameras use convex lenses to focus real images on a piece of film. Both types of images are shown in **Figure 15.**

Figure 15 *Convex lenses can also form real images.*

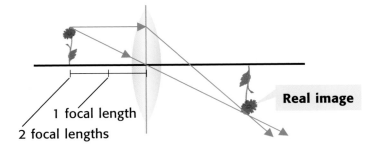

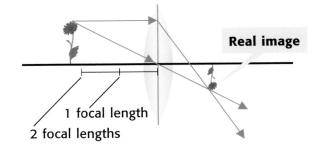

a If the object is located between one and two focal lengths away from the lens, a real, enlarged image is formed far away from the lens. This is how movie projectors produce images on large screens.

b If the object is located more than two focal lengths away from the lens, a real, reduced image is formed close to the lens. This is how the lens of a camera forms images on the film.

Concave Lenses A **concave lens** is thinner in the middle than at the edges. Light rays entering a concave lens parallel to the optical axis always bend away from each other toward the edges of the lens; the rays never meet. Therefore, concave lenses can never form a real image. Instead, they form virtual images, as shown in **Figure 16.** Concave lenses are sometimes combined with other lenses in telescopes. The combination of lenses produces clearer images of distant objects. You will read about another, more common use for concave lenses in the next section.

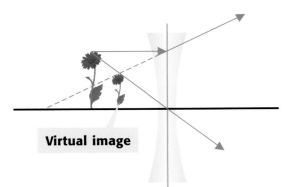

Figure 16 *Concave lenses form reduced virtual images. If you trace the refracted rays in a straight line behind a concave lens, you can determine where the virtual image is formed.*

internet connect

SCI
LINKS
NSTA

TOPIC: Lenses
GO TO: www.scilinks.org
sciLINKS NUMBER: HSTP565

SECTION REVIEW

1. Draw a ray diagram showing how a magnifying glass forms a virtual image.

2. Explain why a concave lens cannot form a real image.

3. **Applying Concepts** Your teacher sometimes uses an overhead projector to show transparencies on a screen. What type of lens does an overhead projector use?

What You'll Do

◆ Identify the parts of the human eye, and describe their functions.
◆ Describe some common vision problems, and explain how they can be corrected.

Light and Sight

When you look around, you can see objects both near and far. You can also see the different colors of the objects. You see luminous objects because they produce their own light, which is detected by your eyes. You see all other objects (illuminated objects) because light reflecting off the objects enters your eyes. But how do your eyes work, and what causes people to have problems with their vision? Read on to find out.

How You Detect Light

Visible light is the part of the electromagnetic spectrum that can be detected by your eyes. The process by which your eye gathers light to form the images that you see involves several steps, as shown in **Figure 17.**

Figure 17 How Your Eyes Work

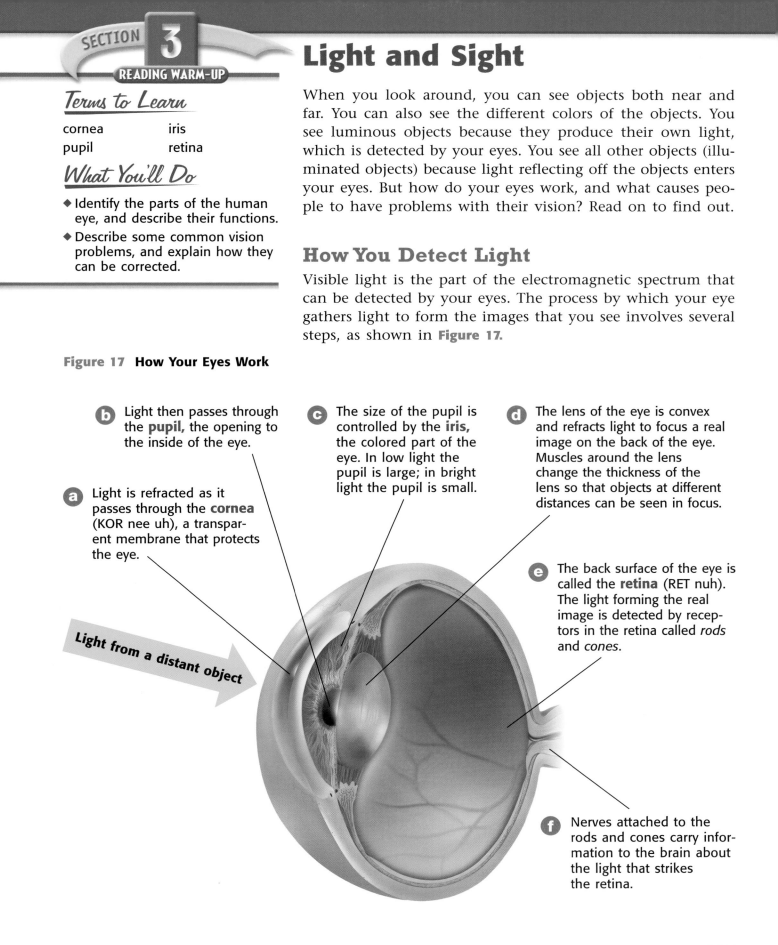

b Light then passes through the **pupil,** the opening to the inside of the eye.

c The size of the pupil is controlled by the **iris,** the colored part of the eye. In low light the pupil is large; in bright light the pupil is small.

d The lens of the eye is convex and refracts light to focus a real image on the back of the eye. Muscles around the lens change the thickness of the lens so that objects at different distances can be seen in focus.

a Light is refracted as it passes through the **cornea** (KOR nee uh), a transparent membrane that protects the eye.

Light from a distant object

e The back surface of the eye is called the **retina** (RET nuh). The light forming the real image is detected by receptors in the retina called *rods* and *cones*.

f Nerves attached to the rods and cones carry information to the brain about the light that strikes the retina.

Common Vision Problems

A person with normal vision can clearly see objects both close up and far away and can distinguish all colors of visible light. However, because the eye is complex, it's no surprise that many people have defects in their eyes that affect their vision. Luckily, some common vision problems can be easily corrected.

Nearsightedness and Farsightedness The lens of a properly working eye focuses light on the retina, so the images formed are always clear. Two common vision problems—nearsightedness and farsightedness—occur when light is not focused on the retina. A nearsighted person can see objects clearly only if the objects are nearby. Objects that are farther away look blurry. A farsighted person can see faraway objects clearly, but objects nearby look blurry. **Figure 18** explains how nearsightedness and farsightedness occur and how they can be corrected.

Figure 18 *Nearsightedness and farsightedness are common vision problems that can be corrected easily with glasses or contact lenses.*

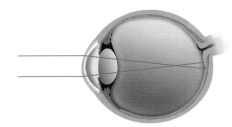 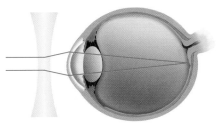

Nearsightedness occurs when the eye is too long and the lens focuses light in front of the retina.

A **concave lens** placed in front of the eye refracts the light outward. The lens in the eye can then focus the light on the retina.

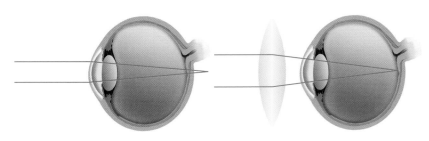

Farsightedness occurs when the eye is too short and the lens focuses light behind the retina.

A **convex lens** placed in front of the eye refracts the light and focuses it slightly. The lens in the eye can then focus the light on the retina.

Color Deficiency Roughly 5 to 8 percent of men and 0.5 percent of women in the world have *color deficiency,* often referred to as colorblindness. True colorblindness, in which a person can see only in black and white, is very rare. The majority of people with color deficiency have trouble distinguishing shades of red and green, or distinguishing red from green.

Color deficiency occurs when the cones in the retina do not receive the right instructions. The three types of cones are named for the colors they detect most—red, green, and blue. Each type of cone reacts to a range of wavelengths of light. A person with normal color vision can see all colors. But in some people, the cones get the wrong instructions and respond to the wrong wavelengths. That person may have trouble seeing certain colors. For example, he or she may see too much red or too much green, and not enough of the other color. **Figure 19** shows one type of test for color deficiency.

Biology
C O N N E C T I O N

Whether a person is colorblind depends on his or her genes. Certain genes give instructions to the cones for detecting certain wavelengths of light. If the genes give the wrong instructions, the person will have a color deficiency. A person needs one set of the genes that give the right instructions. Genes for color vision are on the X chromosome. Women have two X chromosomes, but men have only one. Therefore, men are more likely to be lacking a set of these genes and are more likely than women to be colorblind.

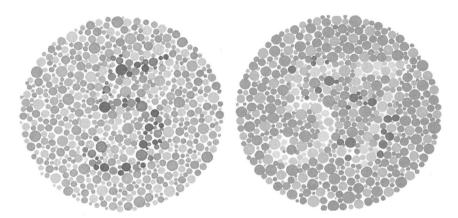

Figure 19 *Doctors use images like these to detect red-green color deficiency. Can you see a number in each image?*

SECTION REVIEW

1. Name the parts of the human eye, and describe what each part does.

2. What kind of lens would help a person who is nearsighted? What kind would help someone who is farsighted?

3. **Inferring Conclusions** Why do you think colorblindness cannot be corrected?

4. **Applying Concepts** Sometimes people are both nearsighted and farsighted. They wear glasses with two different kinds of lenses. Why are two lenses necessary?

☑ internet**connect**

sc*L*INKS
NSTA

TOPIC: The Eye
GO TO: www.scilinks.org
*sci*LINKS NUMBER: HSTP570

SECTION 4

READING WARM-UP

Terms to Learn

laser
hologram

What You'll Do

- Explain how optical instruments use lenses and mirrors to form images.
- Explain how lasers work and what makes laser light different from non-laser light.
- Identify uses for lasers.
- Describe how optical fibers and polarizing filters work.

Light Technology

So far in this chapter, you have learned some ways light can be produced, how mirrors and lenses affect light, and some ways that people use mirrors and lenses. In this section, you will learn how different technological devices rely on mirrors and lenses and how mirrors help produce a type of light called laser light.

Optical Instruments

Optical instruments are devices that use arrangements of mirrors and lenses to help people make observations. Some optical instruments help you see objects that are very far away, and some help you see objects that are very small. Some optical instruments record images. The optical instrument that you are probably most familiar with is the camera.

Cameras The way a camera works is similar to the way your eye works. A camera has a lens that focuses light and has an opening that lets in light. The main difference between a camera and the eye is that the film in a camera permanently stores the images formed on it, but the images formed on the retina disappear when you stop looking at an object. **Figure 20** shows the parts of a camera and their functions.

Figure 20 The Parts of a Camera

The shutter opens and closes behind the lens to control how much light enters the camera. The longer the shutter is open, the more light enters the camera.

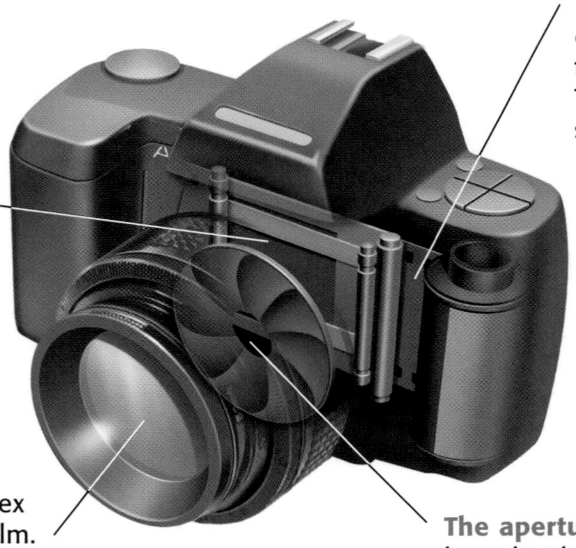

The film is coated with chemicals that react when they are struck by light. The result is an image stored on the film.

The lens of a camera is a convex lens that focuses light on the film. Moving the lens focuses light from objects at different distances.

The aperture is an opening in the lens that lets light into the camera. The larger the aperture is, the more light enters the camera.

Telescopes Astronomers use telescopes to study objects in space, such as the moon, planets, and stars. Telescopes are classified as either refracting or reflecting. Refracting telescopes use lenses to collect light, while reflecting telescopes use mirrors. **Figure 21** illustrates how simple refracting and reflecting telescopes work.

Figure 21 Both refracting and reflecting telescopes are used to see objects that are far away.

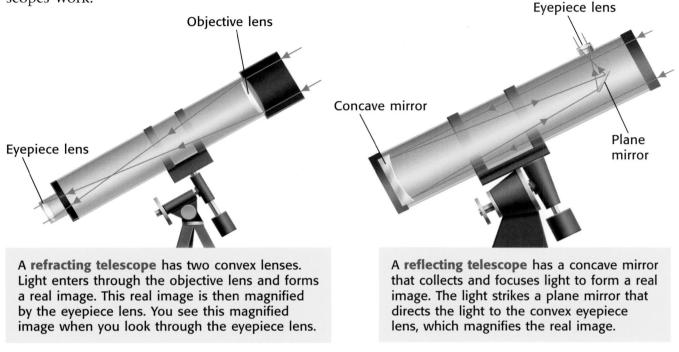

A **refracting telescope** has two convex lenses. Light enters through the objective lens and forms a real image. This real image is then magnified by the eyepiece lens. You see this magnified image when you look through the eyepiece lens.

A **reflecting telescope** has a concave mirror that collects and focuses light to form a real image. The light strikes a plane mirror that directs the light to the convex eyepiece lens, which magnifies the real image.

Light Microscopes Simple light microscopes are similar to refracting telescopes. They have two convex lenses—an objective lens, which is close to the object being studied, and an eyepiece lens, which you look through. The difference between microscopes and telescopes is that microscopes are used to see magnified images of tiny, nearby objects rather than images of large, distant objects.

> ### Self-Check
> Explain why the objective lens of a telescope cannot be a concave lens. *(See page 152 to check your answer.)*

Lasers and Laser Light

Have you ever seen a laser light show? Laser light beams flash through the air and sometimes form pictures on surfaces. A **laser** is a device that produces intense light of only one color and wavelength. Laser light is different from non-laser light in many ways. One important difference is that laser light is *coherent*. When light is coherent, light waves move together as they travel away from their source. The crests and troughs of coherent light waves line up, and the individual waves behave as one single wave. Other differences between laser light and non-laser light are shown in **Figure 22,** on the next page.

Figure 22 Laser Light Versus Non-laser Light

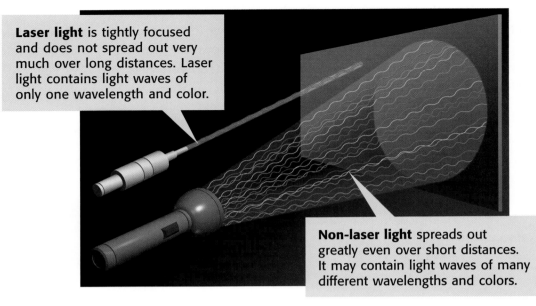

Laser light is tightly focused and does not spread out very much over long distances. Laser light contains light waves of only one wavelength and color.

Non-laser light spreads out greatly even over short distances. It may contain light waves of many different wavelengths and colors.

How Lasers Produce Light The word *laser* stands for light amplification by stimulated emission of radiation. You already know what light and radiation are. *Amplification* is the increase in the brightness of the light.

What is stimulated emission? In an atom, an electron can move from one energy level to another. A photon is released when an electron moves from a higher energy level to a lower energy level. This process is called *emission. Stimulated emission* occurs when a photon strikes an atom in an excited state and makes that atom emit another photon. The newly emitted photon is identical to the first photon, and they travel away from the atom together. **Figure 23** shows how stimulated emission works to produce laser light.

Figure 23 A Helium-Neon Laser

a The inside of the laser is filled with helium and neon gases. An electric current in the gases excites the atoms of the gases.

b Excited neon atoms release photons of red light. When these photons strike other excited neon atoms, stimulated emission occurs.

c Plane mirrors on both ends of the laser reflect photons traveling the length of the laser back and forth along the tube.

d Because the photons travel back and forth many times, many stimulated emissions occur, making the laser light brighter.

e One mirror is only partially coated, so some of the photons "leak" out and form a laser light beam.

Holograms Lasers are used to produce holograms. A **hologram** is a piece of film on which an interference pattern produces a three-dimensional image of an object. You have probably seen holograms on magazine covers or baseball cards. **Figure 24** shows how light from a laser is split into two beams. These two beams combine to form an interference pattern on the film, which results in a hologram.

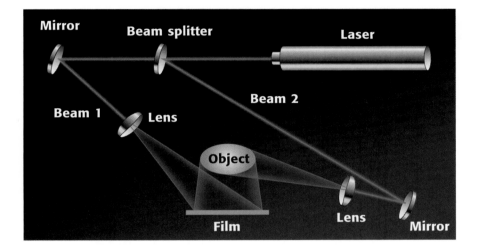

Figure 24 *Light from one beam shines directly on the film, and light from the other beam shines on an object and is reflected onto the film.*

Holograms, like the one shown in **Figure 25,** are similar to photographs because they are images permanently recorded on film. However, unlike photographs, the images you see are not on the surface of the film. They appear either in front of or behind the film. And if you move the image around, you will see it from different angles.

Figure 25 *After the film is developed, the interference pattern reconstructs a three-dimensional image of the object.*

Other Uses for Lasers In addition to making holograms, lasers are used for a wide variety of tasks. For example, lasers are used to cut materials such as metal and cloth. Surgeons sometimes use lasers to cut through human tissue. Laser surgery on the cornea of the eye can correct nearsightedness and farsightedness. And, as you read at the beginning of this chapter, lasers can also be used as extremely accurate rulers. You even use a laser when you listen to music from a CD player.

Fiber Optics

Imagine a glass thread as thin as a human hair that can transmit more than 1,000 telephone conversations at the same time with only flashes of light. It might sound impossible, but such glass threads are at work all over the world. These threads, called *optical fibers,* are thin, flexible glass wires that can transmit light over long distances. Some optical fibers are shown at left. The use of optical fibers is called *fiber optics.* The transmission of information through telephone cables is the most common use of fiber optics. Optical fibers carry information faster and more clearly than older copper telephone cables. Optical fibers are also used to network computers and to allow doctors to see inside patients' bodies without performing major surgery.

Light in a Pipe Optical fibers transmit light over long distances because they act like pipes for light. Just as a good water pipe doesn't let water leak out, a good light pipe doesn't let light leak out. Light stays inside an optical fiber because of total internal reflection. *Total internal reflection* is the complete reflection of light along the inside surface of the medium through which it travels. **Figure 26** shows total internal reflection in an optical fiber.

Figure 26 *As light travels through an optical fiber, it reflects off the sides thousands of times each meter.*

Polarized Light

Next time you go shopping for sunglasses, look for those that have lenses that polarize light. Sunglasses that contain polarizing lenses reduce glare better than sunglasses that do not. *Polarized light* consists of light waves that vibrate in only one plane. **Figure 27** illustrates how light is polarized.

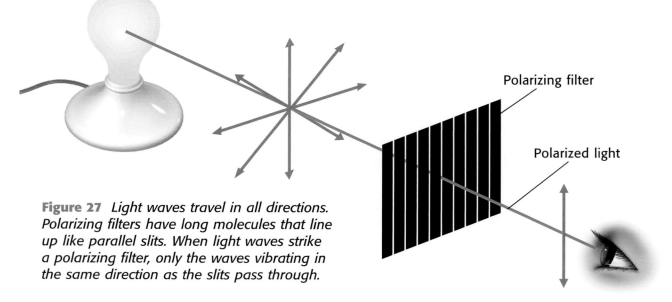

Figure 27 *Light waves travel in all directions. Polarizing filters have long molecules that line up like parallel slits. When light waves strike a polarizing filter, only the waves vibrating in the same direction as the slits pass through.*

When light reflects at a certain angle from a smooth surface, it is completely polarized parallel to that surface. If the surface is parallel to the ground, the light is polarized horizontally. This is what causes the bright glare from bodies of water and car hoods.

Polarizing sunglasses reduce glare from horizontal surfaces because the sunglasses have lenses with vertically polarized filters. These filters allow only vertically vibrating light waves to pass through them. So when you wear polarizing sunglasses, the reflected light that is horizontally polarized does not reach your eyes. Polarizing filters are also used by photographers to reduce glare and reflection in their photographs. Examine **Figure 28** to see the effect of a polarizing filter on a camera.

Now You See, Now You Don't

1. Hold a **lens from a pair of polarizing sunglasses** up to your eye, and look through it. Describe your observations in your ScienceLog.

2. Put a **second polarizing lens** over the first lens. Make sure both lenses are right side up. Look through both lenses, and describe your observations in your ScienceLog.

3. Rotate one lens slowly as you look through both lenses, and describe what happens.

4. Why can't you see through the lenses when they are lined up a certain way? Record your answer in your ScienceLog.

TRY at HOME

Figure 28 *These two photos were taken by the same camera from the same angle. There is less reflected light in the photo at right because a polarizing filter was placed over the lens of the camera.*

SECTION REVIEW

1. How is a camera similar to the human eye?

2. What is the difference between a refracting telescope and a reflecting telescope?

3. How is a beam of laser light different from non-laser light?

4. Why are fiber optics useful for transmitting information?

5. **Applying Concepts** Why do you think lasers are used to cut cloth and metal and to perform surgery?

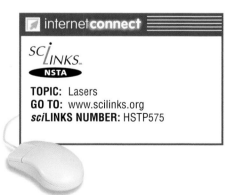

internet**connect**

SC*LINKS*
NSTA

TOPIC: Lasers
GO TO: www.scilinks.org
*sci*LINKS NUMBER: HSTP575

Mirror Images

When light actually passes through an image, the image is a real image. When light does not pass through the image, the image is a virtual image. Recall that plane mirrors produce only virtual images because the image appears to be behind the mirror where no light can pass through it.

In fact, all mirrors can form virtual images, but only some mirrors can form real images. In this experiment, you will explore the virtual images formed by concave and convex mirrors, and you will try to find a real image using both types of mirrors.

MATERIALS

- convex mirror
- concave mirror
- candle
- jar lid
- modeling clay
- matches
- index card

Part A: Finding Virtual Images

Make Observations

1 Hold the convex mirror at arm's length away from your face. Observe the image of your face in the mirror.

2 Slowly move the mirror toward your face, and observe what happens to the image. Record your observations in your ScienceLog.

3 Move the mirror very close to your face. Record your observations in your ScienceLog.

4 Slowly move the mirror away from your face, and observe what happens to the image. Record your observations.

5 Repeat steps 1 through 4 with the concave mirror.

Analyze Your Results

6 For each mirror, did you find a virtual image? How can you tell?

7 Describe the images you found. Were they smaller, larger, or the same size as your face? Were they upright or inverted?

Draw Conclusions

8 Describe at least one use for each type of mirror. Be creative, and try to think of inventions that might use the properties of the two types of mirrors.

Part B: Finding a Real Image

Make Observations

9 In a darkened room, place a candle in a jar lid near one end of a table. Use modeling clay to hold the candle in place. Light the candle.
Caution: Use extreme care around an open flame.

10 Use more modeling clay to make a base to hold the convex mirror upright. Place the mirror at the other end of the table, facing the candle.

11 Hold the index card between the candle and the mirror but slightly to one side so that you do not block the candlelight, as shown below.

12 Move the card slowly from side to side and back and forth to see whether you can focus an image of the candle on it. Record your results in your ScienceLog.

13 Repeat steps 10–12 with the concave mirror.

Analyze Your Results

14 For each mirror, did you find a real image? How can you tell?

15 Describe the real image you found. Was it smaller, larger, or the same size as the object? Was it upright or inverted?

Draw Conclusions

16 Astronomical telescopes use large mirrors to reflect light to form a real image. Based on your results, would a concave or convex mirror be better for this instrument? Explain your answer.

Chapter Highlights

SECTION 1

Vocabulary

luminous *(p. 94)*

illuminated *(p. 94)*

incandescent light *(p. 95)*

fluorescent light *(p. 96)*

neon light *(p. 96)*

vapor light *(p. 97)*

Section Notes

• You see objects either because they are luminous (produce their own light) or because they are illuminated (reflect light).

• Light produced by hot objects is incandescent light. Ordinary light bulbs are a common source of incandescent light.

• Fluorescent light is visible light emitted by a particle when it absorbs ultraviolet light. Little energy is wasted by fluorescent light bulbs.

• Neon light results from an electric current in certain gases.

• Vapor light is produced when electrons combine with gaseous metal atoms.

SECTION 2

Vocabulary

plane mirror *(p. 99)*

concave mirror *(p. 100)*

focal point *(p. 100)*

convex mirror *(p. 102)*

lens *(p. 103)*

convex lens *(p. 103)*

concave lens *(p. 104)*

Section Notes

• Rays are arrows that show the path and direction of a single light wave. Ray diagrams can be used to determine where images are formed by mirrors and lenses.

• Plane mirrors produce virtual images that are the same size as the objects. These images are reversed left to right.

☑ Skills Check

Visual Understanding

OPTICAL AXIS, FOCAL POINT, AND FOCAL LENGTH To understand how concave and convex mirrors and lenses work, you need to know what the terms *optical axis*, *focal point*, and *focal length* mean. Figure 10 on page 100 explains these terms.

LASERS Laser light is different from ordinary non-laser light in several ways. Look back at Figure 22 on page 110 to review some differences between the two types of light.

THE EYE Study Figure 17 on page 105 to review the parts of the eye and review the process by which your eye gathers light to form the images that you see.

SECTION 2

- Concave mirrors can produce real images and virtual images. They can also be used to produce a powerful light beam.

- Convex mirrors produce only virtual images.

- Convex lenses can produce real images and virtual images. A magnifying glass is an example of a convex lens.

- Concave lenses produce only virtual images.

Labs

Images from Convex Lenses *(p. 134)*

SECTION 3

Vocabulary

cornea *(p. 105)*
pupil *(p. 105)*
iris *(p. 105)*
retina *(p. 105)*

Section Notes

- Your eye has several parts, such as the cornea, the pupil, the iris, the lens, and the retina.

- Nearsightedness and farsightedness occur when light is not focused on the retina. Both problems can be corrected with glasses or contact lenses.

- Color deficiency is a genetic condition in which cones in the retina are given the wrong instructions. Color deficiency cannot be corrected.

SECTION 4

Vocabulary

laser *(p. 109)*
hologram *(p. 111)*

Section Notes

- Optical instruments, such as cameras, telescopes, and microscopes, are devices that use mirrors and lenses to help people make observations.

- Lasers are devices that produce intense, coherent light of only one wavelength and color. Lasers produce light by a process called stimulated emission.

- Optical fibers can transmit light over long distances because of total internal reflection.

- Polarized light contains light waves that vibrate in only one direction.

---

internet connect

GO TO: go.hrw.com

Visit the **HRW** Web site for a variety of learning tools related to this chapter. Just type in the keyword:

KEYWORD: HSTLOW

GO TO: www.scilinks.org

Visit the **National Science Teachers Association** on-line Web site for Internet resources related to this chapter. Just type in the *sci*LINKS number for more information about the topic:

TOPIC: Producing Light	*sci*LINKS NUMBER: HSTP555
TOPIC: Mirrors	*sci*LINKS NUMBER: HSTP560
TOPIC: Lenses	*sci*LINKS NUMBER: HSTP565
TOPIC: The Eye	*sci*LINKS NUMBER: HSTP570
TOPIC: Lasers	*sci*LINKS NUMBER: HSTP575

Chapter Review

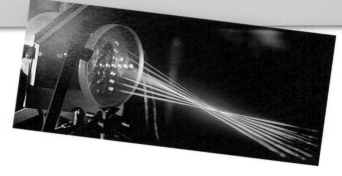

To complete the following sentences, choose the correct term from each pair of terms listed below:

1. ___?___ is commonly used in homes and produces a lot of thermal energy. *(Incandescent light* or *Fluorescent light)*

2. A ___?___ is curved inward, like the inside of a spoon. *(convex mirror* or *concave mirror)*

3. You can see an object when light is focused on the ___?___ of your eye. *(pupil* or *retina)*

4. A ___?___ is a device that produces coherent, intense light of only one color. *(laser* or *lens)*

5. You can see this book because it is a(n) ___?___ object. *(luminous* or *illuminated)*

UNDERSTANDING CONCEPTS

Multiple Choice

6. When you look at yourself in a plane mirror, you see a
   a. real image behind the mirror.
   b. real image on the surface of the mirror.
   c. virtual image that appears to be behind the mirror.
   d. virtual image that appears to be in front of the mirror.

7. A vision problem that occurs when light is focused in front of the retina is
   a. nearsightedness.
   b. farsightedness.
   c. color deficiency.
   d. None of the above

8. Which part of the eye refracts light?
   a. iris   c. lens
   b. cornea   d. both (b) and (c)

9. Visible light produced when electrons combine with gaseous metal atoms is
   a. incandescent light.
   b. fluorescent light.
   c. neon light.
   d. vapor light.

10. You see less of a glare when you wear certain sunglasses because the lenses
    a. produce total internal reflection.
    b. create holograms.
    c. produce coherent light.
    d. polarize light.

11. What kind of mirrors provide images of large areas and are used for security?
    a. plane mirrors   c. convex mirrors
    b. concave mirrors   d. all of the above

12. A simple refracting telescope has
    a. a convex lens and a concave lens.
    b. a concave mirror and a convex lens.
    c. two convex lenses.
    d. two concave lenses.

13. Light waves in a laser beam interact and act as one wave. This light is called
    a. red.   c. coherent.
    b. white.   d. emitted.

Short Answer

14. What type of lens should be prescribed for a person who cannot focus on nearby objects? Explain.

15. How is a hologram different from a photograph?

16. Why might a scientist at the North Pole need polarizing sunglasses?

Concept Mapping

17. Use the following terms to create a concept map: lens, telescope, camera, real image, virtual image, optical instrument.

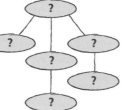

CRITICAL THINKING AND PROBLEM SOLVING

18. Stoplights are usually mounted so that the red light is on the top and the green light is on the bottom. Explain why it is important for a person who has red-green color deficiency to know this arrangement.

19. Some companies are producing fluorescent light bulbs that will fit into sockets on lamps designed for incandescent light bulbs. Although fluorescent bulbs are more expensive, the companies hope that people will use them because they are better for the environment. Explain why fluorescent light bulbs are better for the environment than incandescent light bulbs.

20. Imagine you are given a small device that produces a beam of red light. You want to find out if the device is producing laser light or if it is just a red flashlight. To do this, you point the beam of light against a wall across the room. What would you expect to see if the device is producing laser light? Explain.

INTERPRETING GRAPHICS

21. Examine the ray diagrams below, and identify the type of mirror or lens that is being used and the kind of image that is being formed.

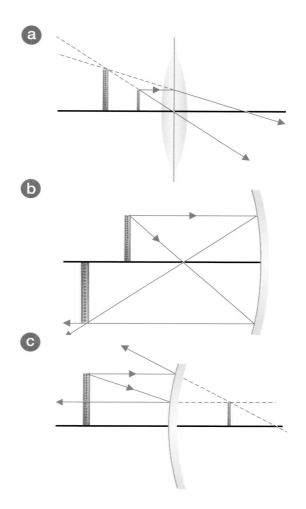

Reading Check-up Take a minute to review your answers to the Pre-Reading Questions found at the bottom of page 92. Have your answers changed? If necessary, revise your answers based on what you have learned since you began this chapter.

Science, Technology, and Society

Traffic Lights

One day in the 1920s, an automobile collided with a horse and carriage. The riders were thrown from their carriage, the driver of the car was knocked unconscious, and the horse was fatally injured. A man named Garrett Morgan (1877–1963) witnessed this scene, and the accident gave him an idea.

A Bright Idea

Morgan's idea was a signal that included signs to direct traffic at busy intersections. The signal could be seen from a distance and could be clearly understood.

Morgan patented the first traffic signal in 1923. His signal looked very different from those used today. Unlike the small, three-bulb signal boxes that now hang over most busy intersections, the early versions were T-shaped, with the words *stop* and *go* printed on them.

Morgan's traffic signal was operated by a preset timing system. An electric motor turned a system of gears that operated a timing dial. As the timing dial rotated, it turned the switches on and off.

Morgan's invention was an immediate success, and he sold the patent to General Electric Corporation for $40,000—quite a large sum in those days. Since then, later versions of Morgan's traffic signal have been the mainstay of urban traffic control.

Light Technology

The technology of traffic lights continues to improve. For example, in some newer models the timing can be changed, depending on the traffic needs for a particular time of day. Some models have sensors installed in the street to monitor traffic flow. In other models, sensors can be triggered from inside an ambulance so that the light automatically turns green, allowing the ambulance to pass.

More About Morgan

Garrett Morgan, the son of former slaves, was born in Paris, Kentucky. He was one of 11 children, and his formal education ended at the sixth grade. At age 14, with no money and few skills, Morgan left home to work in Cincinnati, Ohio. He soon moved to Cleveland and quickly taught himself enough about sewing machines to get a job repairing them. Morgan saw how important the rest of his education was, so he taught himself and he hired tutors to help him complete his education. By 1907, Morgan opened his own sewing-machine repair shop. He was on his way!

Not only was Morgan an inventor, he was a hero. Gas masks that Morgan invented in 1912 were used in WWI to protect soldiers from chlorine gas fumes. Morgan himself, wearing one of his masks, later helped save several men trapped in a tunnel after a gas explosion.

Think About It

▶ Traffic control is not the only system in which light is used as a signal. What are some other systems that do so, and what makes light so useful for communication?

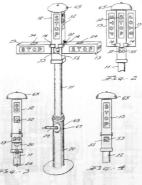

▲ *Morgan's patent for the first traffic light*

EYE ON THE ENVIRONMENT

Light Pollution

At night, large cities are often visible from far away. Soft light from windows outlines buildings. Bright lights from stadiums and parking lots shine like beacons. Scattered house lights twinkle like jewels. The sight is stunning!

Unfortunately, astronomers consider all these lights a form of pollution. Around the world, light pollution is reducing astronomers' ability to see beyond our atmosphere.

Sky Glow

Twenty years ago, stars were very visible above even large cities. The stars are still there, but now they are obscured by city lights. This glow, called sky glow, is created when light reflects off dust and other particles suspended in the atmosphere. Sky glow affects the entire atmosphere to some degree. Today, even remote locations around the globe are affected by light pollution.

The majority of light pollution comes from outdoor lights such as headlights, street lights, porch lights, and bright parking-lot and stadium lights. Other sources include forest fires and gas burn-offs in oil fields. Air pollution makes the situation worse, adding more particles to the air so that reflection is even greater.

A Light of Hope

Unlike other kinds of pollution, light pollution has some simple solutions. In fact, light pollution can be reduced in as little time as it takes to turn off a light! While turning off most city lights is impractical, several simple strategies can make a surprising difference. For example, using covered outdoor lights keeps the light angled downward, preventing most of the light from reaching particles in the sky. Also, using motion-sensitive lights and timed lights helps eliminate unnecessary light.

▲ *Lights from cities can be seen from space, as shown in this photograph taken from the space shuttle* Columbia. *Bright, uncovered lights (inset) create a glowing haze in the night sky above most cities in the United States.*

Many of these strategies also save money by saving energy.

Astronomers hope that public awareness will help improve the visibility of the night sky in and around major cities. Some cities, including Boston and Tucson, have already made some progress in reducing light pollution. Scientists have projected that if left unchecked, light pollution will affect every observatory on Earth within the next decade.

See for Yourself

▶ With your parents' permission, go outside at night and find a place where you can see the sky. Count the number of stars you can see. Now turn on a flashlight or porch light. How many stars can you see now? Compare your results. How much was your visibility reduced?

Exploring, inventing, and investigating are essential to the study of science. However, these activities can also be dangerous. To make sure that your experiments and explorations are safe, you must be aware of a variety of safety guidelines.

You have probably heard of the saying, "It is better to be safe than sorry." This is particularly true in a science classroom where experiments and explorations are being performed. Being uninformed and careless can result in serious injuries. Don't take chances with your own safety or with anyone else's.

Following are important guidelines for staying safe in the science classroom. Your teacher may also have safety guidelines and tips that are specific to your classroom and laboratory. Take the time to be safe.

Safety Rules!

Start Out Right

Always get your teacher's permission before attempting any laboratory exploration. Read the procedures carefully, and pay particular attention to safety information and caution statements. If you are unsure about what a safety symbol means, look it up or ask your teacher. You cannot be too careful when it comes to safety. If an accident does occur, inform your teacher immediately, regardless of how minor you think the accident is.

Safety Symbols

All of the experiments and investigations in this book and their related worksheets include important safety symbols to alert you to particular safety concerns. Become familiar with these symbols so that when you see them, you will know what they mean and what to do. It is important that you read this entire safety section to learn about specific dangers in the laboratory.

If you are instructed to note the odor of a substance, wave the fumes toward your nose with your hand. Never put your nose close to the source.

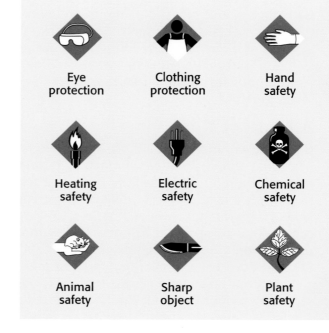

Eye protection	Clothing protection	Hand safety
Heating safety	Electric safety	Chemical safety
Animal safety	Sharp object	Plant safety

Eye Safety

Wear safety goggles when working around chemicals, acids, bases, or any type of flame or heating device. Wear safety goggles any time there is even the slightest chance that harm could come to your eyes. If any substance gets into your eyes, notify your teacher immediately, and flush your eyes with running water for at least 15 minutes. Treat any unknown chemical as if it were a dangerous chemical. Never look directly into the sun. Doing so could cause permanent blindness.

Avoid wearing contact lenses in a laboratory situation. Even if you are wearing safety goggles, chemicals can get between the contact lenses and your eyes. If your doctor requires that you wear contact lenses instead of glasses, wear eye-cup safety goggles in the lab.

Safety Equipment

Know the locations of the nearest fire alarms and any other safety equipment, such as fire blankets and eyewash fountains, as identified by your teacher, and know the procedures for using them.

Be extra careful when using any glassware. When adding a heavy object to a graduated cylinder, tilt the cylinder so the object slides slowly to the bottom.

Neatness

Keep your work area free of all unnecessary books and papers. Tie back long hair, and secure loose sleeves or other loose articles of clothing, such as ties and bows. Remove dangling jewelry. Don't wear open-toed shoes or sandals in the laboratory. Never eat, drink, or apply cosmetics in a laboratory setting. Food, drink, and cosmetics can easily become contaminated with dangerous materials.

Certain hair products (such as aerosol hair spray) are flammable and should not be worn while working near an open flame. Avoid wearing hair spray or hair gel on lab days.

Sharp/Pointed Objects

Use knives and other sharp instruments with extreme care. Never cut objects while holding them in your hands. Place objects on a suitable work surface for cutting.

Heat

Wear safety goggles when using a heating device or a flame. Whenever possible, use an electric hot plate as a heat source instead of an open flame. When heating materials in a test tube, always angle the test tube away from yourself and others. In order to avoid burns, wear heat-resistant gloves whenever instructed to do so.

Electricity

Be careful with electrical cords. When using a microscope with a lamp, do not place the cord where it could trip someone. Do not let cords hang over a table edge in a way that could cause equipment to fall if the cord is accidentally pulled. Do not use equipment with damaged cords. Be sure your hands are dry and that the electrical equipment is in the "off" position before plugging it in. Turn off and unplug electrical equipment when you are finished.

Chemicals

Wear safety goggles when handling any potentially dangerous chemicals, acids, or bases. If a chemical is unknown, handle it as you would a dangerous chemical. Wear an apron and safety gloves when working with acids or bases or whenever you are told to do so. If a spill gets on your skin or clothing, rinse it off immediately with water for at least 5 minutes while calling to your teacher.

Never mix chemicals unless your teacher tells you to do so. Never taste, touch, or smell chemicals unless you are specifically directed to do so. Before working with a flammable liquid or gas, check for the presence of any source of flame, spark, or heat.

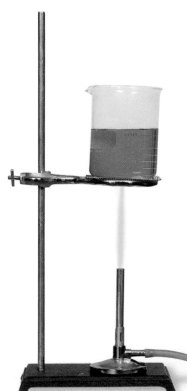

Animal Safety

Always obtain your teacher's permission before bringing any animal into the school building. Handle animals only as your teacher directs. Always treat animals carefully and with respect. Wash your hands thoroughly after handling any animal.

Plant Safety

Do not eat any part of a plant or plant seed used in the laboratory. Wash hands thoroughly after handling any part of a plant. When in nature, do not pick any wild plants unless your teacher instructs you to do so.

Glassware

Examine all glassware before use. Be sure that glassware is clean and free of chips and cracks. Report damaged glassware to your teacher. Glass containers used for heating should be made of heat-resistant glass.

Wave Speed, Frequency, and Wavelength

Wave speed, frequency, and wavelength are three related properties of waves. In this lab you will make observations and collect data to determine the relationship among these properties.

Part A—Wave Speed

Procedure

1. Copy Table 1 into your ScienceLog.

Table 1 Wave Speed Data			
Trial	Length of spring (m)	Time for wave (s)	Speed of wave (m/s)
1			
2			
3			
Average			

DO NOT WRITE IN BOOK

2. On the floor or a table, two students should stretch the spring to a length of 2 to 4 m. A third student should measure the length of the spring. Record the length in Table 1.

3. One student should pull part of the spring sideways with one hand, as shown at right, and release the pulled-back portion. This will cause a wave to travel down the spring.

4. Using a stopwatch, the third student should measure how long it takes for the wave to travel down the length of the spring and back. Record this time in Table 1.

5. Repeat steps 3 and 4 two more times.

Analyze Your Results

6. Calculate and record the wave speed for each trial. (Hint: Speed equals distance divided by time; distance is twice the spring length.)

7. Calculate and record the average time and the average wave speed.

Materials

- coiled spring toy
- meterstick
- stopwatch

Part B—Wavelength and Frequency

Procedure

8. Keep the spring the same length that you used in Part A.

9. Copy Table 2 into your ScienceLog.

Table 2 Wavelength and Frequency Data				
Trial	Length of spring (m)	Time for 10 cycles (s)	Wave frequency (Hz)	Wavelength (m)
1				
2				
3				
Average				

DO NOT WRITE IN BOOK

10. One of the two students holding the spring should start shaking the spring from side to side until a wave pattern appears that resembles one of those shown below.

11. Using the stopwatch, the third group member should measure and record how long it takes for 10 cycles of the wave pattern to occur. (One back-and-forth shake is one cycle.) Keep the pattern going so that measurements for three trials can be made.

Analyze Your Results

12. Calculate the frequency for each trial by dividing the number of cycles (10) by the time. Record the answers in Table 2.

13. Determine the wavelength using the equation at right that matches your wave pattern. Record your answer in Table 2.

14. Calculate and record the average time and frequency.

Draw Conclusions—Parts A and B

15. To discover the relationship among speed, wavelength, and frequency, try multiplying or dividing any two of them to see if the result equals the third. (Use the average speed, wavelength, and average frequency from your data tables.) In your ScienceLog, write the equation that shows the relationship.

16. Reread the definitions for *frequency* and *wavelength* in the chapter titled "The Energy of Waves." Use these definitions to explain the relationship that you discovered.

Wave Patterns

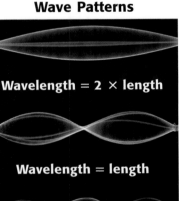

Wavelength = 2 × length

Wavelength = length

Wavelength = 2/3 × length

Easy Listening

Pitch describes how low or high a sound is. A sound's pitch is related to its frequency—the number of waves per second. Frequency is expressed in hertz (Hz), where 1 Hz equals one wave per second. Most humans can hear frequencies from 20 Hz to 20,000 Hz. However, not everyone detects all pitches equally well at all distances. In this activity you will collect data to see how well you and your classmates hear different frequencies at different distances.

Materials

- 4 tuning forks of different frequencies
- pink rubber eraser
- meterstick
- graph paper

Ask a Question

1. Do students in your classroom hear low-, mid-, or high-frequency sounds better?

Form a Hypothesis

2. In your ScienceLog, write a hypothesis that answers the question above. Explain your reasoning.

Test the Hypothesis

3. Choose one member of your group to be the sound maker. The others will be the listeners.

4. Copy the data table below into your ScienceLog. Be sure to include a column for every listener in your group.

Data Collection Table				
	Distance (m)			
Frequency	Listener 1	Listener 2	Listener 3	Average
1 (___Hz)				
2 (___Hz)				
3 (___Hz)		DO NOT WRITE IN BOOK		
4 (___Hz)				

5. Record the frequency of one of the tuning forks in the top row of the first column of the data table.

6. The listeners should stand in front of the sound maker with their backs turned.

7. The sound maker will create a sound by striking the tip of the tuning fork gently with the eraser.

8. The listeners who hear the sound should take one step away from the sound maker. The listeners who do not hear the sound should stay where they are.

9. Repeat steps 7 and 8 until none of the listeners can hear the sound or the listeners reach the edge of the room.

10. Using the meterstick, the sound maker should measure the distance from his or her position to each of the listeners. All group members should record this data in their tables.

11. Repeat steps 5 through 10 with a different tuning fork.

12. Continue until all four tuning forks have been tested.

Analyze the Results

13. Calculate the average distance for each frequency. Share your group's data with the rest of the class to make a data table for the whole class.

14. Calculate the average distance for each frequency for the class.

15. Make a graph of the class results, plotting average distance (y-axis) versus frequency (x-axis).

Draw Conclusions

16. Was everyone in the class able to hear all frequencies equally? (Hint: Was the average distance for each frequency the same?)

17. If the answer to question 16 is no, which frequency had the largest average distance? Which frequency had the smallest average distance?

18. Based on your graph, do your results support your hypothesis? Explain your answer.

19. Do you think your class sample is large enough to confirm your hypothesis for all humans of all ages? Explain your answer.

The Speed of Sound

In the chapter titled "The Nature of Sound," you learned that the speed of sound in air is 343 m/s at 20°C (approximately room temperature). In this lab you'll design an experiment to measure the speed of sound yourself—and you'll determine if you're "up to speed"!

Materials

- materials of your choice, approved by your teacher

Procedure

1. Brainstorm with your teammates to come up with a way to measure the speed of sound. Consider the following as you design your experiment:

   a. You must have a method of making a sound. Some simple examples include speaking, clapping your hands, and hitting two boards together.

   b. Remember that speed is equal to distance divided by time. You must devise methods to measure the distance that a sound travels and to measure the amount of time it takes for that sound to travel that distance.

   c. Sound travels very rapidly. A sound from across the room will reach your ears almost before you can start recording the time! You may wish to have the sound travel a long distance.

   d. Remember that sound travels in waves. Think about the interactions of sound waves. You might be able to include these interactions in your design.

2. Discuss your experimental design with your teacher, including any equipment you need. Your teacher may have questions that will help you improve your design.

Conduct an Experiment

3. Once your design is approved, carry out your experiment. Be sure to perform several trials. Record your results in your ScienceLog.

Draw Conclusions

4. Was your result close to the value given in the introduction to this lab? If not, what factors may have caused you to get such a different value?

5. Why was it important for you to perform several trials in your experiment?

Communicate Your Results

6. Compare your results with those of your classmates. Determine which experimental design provided the best results. In your ScienceLog, explain why you think this design was so successful.

Tuneful Tube

If you have seen a singer shatter a crystal glass simply by singing a note, you have seen an example of resonance. For this to happen, the note has to match the resonant frequency of the glass. A column of air within a cylinder can also resonate if the air column is the proper length for the frequency of the note. In this lab you will investigate the relationship between the length of an air column, the frequency, and the wavelength during resonance.

Materials

- 100 mL graduated cylinder
- water
- plastic tube, supplied by your teacher
- metric ruler
- 4 tuning forks of different frequencies
- pink rubber eraser
- graph paper

Procedure

1. Copy the data table below into your ScienceLog.

Data Collection Table				
Frequency (Hz)				
Length (cm)				

DO NOT WRITE IN BOOK

2. Fill the graduated cylinder with water.

3. Hold a plastic tube in the water so that about 3 cm is above the water.

4. Record the frequency of the first tuning fork. Gently strike the tuning fork with the eraser, and hold it so that the prongs are just above the tube, as shown at right. Slowly move the tube and fork up and down until you hear the loudest sound.

5. Measure the distance from the top of the tube to the water. Record this length in your data table.

6. Repeat steps 3–5 using the other three tuning forks.

Analysis

7. Calculate the wavelength (in centimeters) of each sound wave by dividing the speed of sound in air (343 m/s at 20°C) by the frequency and multiplying by 100.

8. Make the following graphs: air column length versus frequency and wavelength versus frequency. On both graphs, plot the frequency on the x-axis.

9. Describe the trend between the length of the air column and the frequency of the tuning fork.

10. How are the pitches you heard related to the wavelengths of the sounds?

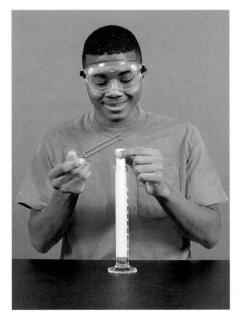

DISCOVERY LAB

What Color of Light Is Best for Green Plants?

Plants grow well outdoors under natural sunlight. However, some plants are grown indoors under artificial light. A wide variety of colored lights are available for helping plants grow indoors. In this experiment, you'll test several colors of light to discover which color best meets the energy needs of green plants.

Materials

- masking tape
- marker
- Petri dishes and covers
- water
- paper towels
- bean seedlings
- variety of colored lights, supplied by your teacher

Ask a Question

1. What color of light is the best for growing green plants?

Form a Hypothesis

2. In your ScienceLog, write a hypothesis that answers the question above. Explain your reasoning.

Test the Hypothesis

3. Use the masking tape and marker to label the side of each Petri dish with your name and the type of light you will place the dish under.

4. Place a moist paper towel in each Petri dish. Place five seedlings on top of the paper towel. Cover each dish.

5. Record your observations of the seedlings, such as length, color, and number of leaves, in your ScienceLog.

6. Place each dish under the appropriate light.

7. Observe the Petri dishes every day for at least 5 days. Record your observations in your ScienceLog.

Analyze the Results

8. Based on your results, which color of light is the best for growing green plants? Which color of light is the worst?

Draw Conclusions

9. Remember that the color of an opaque object (such as a plant) is determined by the colors the object reflects. Use this information to explain your answer to question 8.

10. Would a purple light be good for growing purple plants? Explain.

Communicate Results

11. Write a short paragraph summarizing your conclusions.

Which Color Is Hottest?

Will a navy blue hat or a white hat keep your head warmer in cool weather? Colored objects absorb energy, which can make the objects warmer. How much energy is absorbed depends on the object's color. In this experiment you will test several colors under a bright light to determine which colors absorb the most energy.

Materials

- tape
- squares of colored paper
- thermometer
- light source
- cup of room-temperature water
- paper towels
- graph paper
- colored pencils or pens

Procedure

1. Copy the table below into your ScienceLog. Be sure to have one column for each color of paper you have and enough rows to end at 3 minutes.

Data Collection Table				
Time (s)	White	Red	Blue	Black
0				
15				
30				
45				
etc.				

DO NOT WRITE IN BOOK

2. Tape a piece of colored paper around the bottom of a thermometer and hold it under the light source. Record the temperature every 15 seconds for 3 minutes.

3. Cool the thermometer by removing the piece of paper and placing the thermometer in the cup of room-temperature water. After 1 minute, remove the thermometer, and dry it with a paper towel.

4. Repeat steps 2 and 3 with each color, making sure to hold the thermometer at the same distance from the light source.

Analyze the Results

5. Prepare a graph of temperature (*y*-axis) versus time (*x*-axis). Plot all data on one graph using a different colored pencil or pen for each set of data.

6. Rank the colors you used in order from hottest to coolest.

Draw Conclusions

7. Compare the colors based on the amount of energy each absorbs.

8. In this experiment a white light was used. How would your results be different if you used a red light? Explain.

9. Use the relationship between color and energy absorbed to explain why different colors of clothing are used for different seasons.

133

Images from Convex Lenses

A convex lens is thicker in the center than at the edges. Light rays passing through a convex lens come together at a point. Under certain conditions, a convex lens will create a real image of an object. This image will have certain characteristics, depending on the distance between the object and the lens. In this experiment you will determine the characteristics of real images created by a convex lens—the kind of lens used as a magnifying lens.

Materials

- index card
- modeling clay
- candle
- jar lid
- matches
- convex lens
- meterstick

Ask a Question

1. What are the characteristics of real images created by a convex lens? How do these characteristics depend on the location of the object and the lens?

Conduct an Experiment

2. Copy the table below into your ScienceLog.

		Data Collection		
Image	**Orientation (upright/inverted)**	**Size (larger/smaller)**	**Image distance (cm)**	**Object distance (cm)**
1				
2				
3				

3. Use some modeling clay to make a base for the lens. Place the lens and base in the middle of the table.

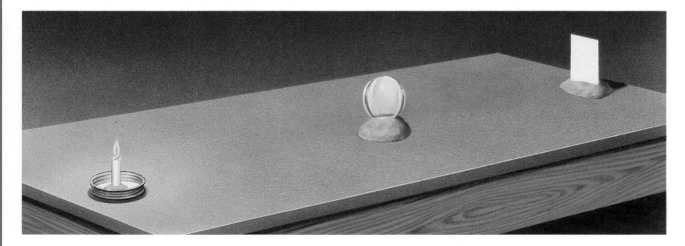

4. Stand the index card upright in some modeling clay on one side of the lens.

5. Place the candle in the jar lid, and anchor it with some modeling clay. Place the candle on the table so that the lens is halfway between the candle and the card. Light the candle. **Caution:** Use extreme care around an open flame.

Collect Data

6. In a darkened room, slowly move the card and the candle away from the lens while keeping the lens exactly halfway between the card and the candle. Continue until you see a clear image of the candle flame on the card. This is image 1.

7. Measure and record the distance between the lens and the card (image distance) and between the lens and the candle (object distance).

8. Is image 1 upright or inverted? Is it larger or smaller than the candle? Record this information in the table.

9. Slide the lens toward the candle to get a new image (image 2) of the candle on the card. Leave the lens in this position.

10. Repeat steps 7 and 8 for image 2.

11. Move the lens back to the middle, and then move the lens toward the card to get a third image (image 3).

12. Repeat steps 7 and 8 for image 3.

Analyze Your Results

13. Describe the trend between image distance and image size.

14. What are the similarities between the real images formed by a convex lens?

Draw Conclusions

15. The lens of your eye is a convex lens. Use the information you collected to describe the image projected on the back of your eye when you look at an object.

16. Convex lenses are used in film projectors. Explain why your favorite movie stars are truly "larger than life" on the screen in terms of the image distance and the object distance.

Communicate Your Results

17. Write a paragraph to summarize your answer to the question in step 1. Be sure to include the roles that image distance and object distance have in determining the characteristics of the images.

Concept Mapping: A Way to Bring Ideas Together

What Is a Concept Map?

Have you ever tried to tell someone about a book or a chapter you've just read and found that you can remember only a few isolated words and ideas? Or maybe you've memorized facts for a test and then weeks later discovered you're not even sure what topics those facts covered.

In both cases, you may have understood the ideas or concepts by themselves but not in relation to one another. If you could somehow link the ideas together, you would probably understand them better and remember them longer. This is something a concept map can help you do. A concept map is a way to see how ideas or concepts fit together. It can help you see the "big picture."

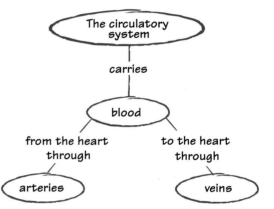

How to Make a Concept Map

1 Make a list of the main ideas or concepts.

It might help to write each concept on its own slip of paper. This will make it easier to rearrange the concepts as many times as necessary to make sense of how the concepts are connected. After you've made a few concept maps this way, you can go directly from writing your list to actually making the map.

2 Arrange the concepts in order from the most general to the most specific.

Put the most general concept at the top and circle it. Ask yourself, "How does this concept relate to the remaining concepts?" As you see the relationships, arrange the concepts in order from general to specific.

3 Connect the related concepts with lines.

4 On each line, write an action word or short phrase that shows how the concepts are related.

Look at the concept maps on this page, and then see if you can make one for the following terms:

plants, water, photosynthesis, carbon dioxide, sun's energy

One possible answer is provided at right, but don't look at it until you try the concept map yourself.

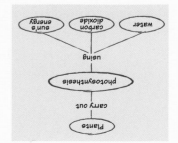

SI Measurement

The International System of Units, or SI, is the standard system of measurement used by many scientists. Using the same standards of measurement makes it easier for scientists to communicate with one another.

SI works by combining prefixes and base units. Each base unit can be used with different prefixes to define smaller and larger quantities. The table below lists common SI prefixes.

SI Prefixes			
Prefix	**Abbreviation**	**Factor**	**Example**
kilo-	k	1,000	kilogram, 1 kg = 1,000 g
hecto-	h	100	hectoliter, 1 hL = 100 L
deka-	da	10	dekameter, 1 dam = 10 m
		1	meter, liter
deci-	d	0.1	decigram, 1 dg = 0.1 g
centi-	c	0.01	centimeter, 1 cm = 0.01 m
milli-	m	0.001	milliliter, 1 mL = 0.001 L
micro-	µ	0.000 001	micrometer, 1 µm = 0.000 001 m

SI Conversion Table		
SI units	**From SI to English**	**From English to SI**
Length		
kilometer (km) = 1,000 m	1 km = 0.621 mi	1 mi = 1.609 km
meter (m) = 100 cm	1 m = 3.281 ft	1 ft = 0.305 m
centimeter (cm) = 0.01 m	1 cm = 0.394 in.	1 in. = 2.540 cm
millimeter (mm) = 0.001 m	1 mm = 0.039 in.	
micrometer (µm) = 0.000 001 m		
nanometer (nm) = 0.000 000 001 m		
Area		
square kilometer (km^2) = 100 hectares	1 km^2 = 0.386 mi^2	1 mi^2 = 2.590 km^2
hectare (ha) = 10,000 m^2	1 ha = 2.471 acres	1 acre = 0.405 ha
square meter (m^2) = 10,000 cm^2	1 m^2 = 10.765 ft^2	1 ft^2 = 0.093 m^2
square centimeter (cm^2) = 100 mm^2	1 cm^2 = 0.155 in.^{2}	1 in.^{2} = 6.452 cm^2
Volume		
liter (L) = 1,000 mL = 1 dm^3	1 L = 1.057 fl qt	1 fl qt = 0.946 L
milliliter (mL) = 0.001 L = 1 cm^3	1 mL = 0.034 fl oz	1 fl oz = 29.575 mL
microliter (µL) = 0.000 001 L		
Mass		
kilogram (kg) = 1,000 g	1 kg = 2.205 lb	1 lb = 0.454 kg
gram (g) = 1,000 mg	1 g = 0.035 oz	1 oz = 28.349 g
milligram (mg) = 0.001 g		
microgram (µg) = 0.000 001 g		

Scientific Method

The series of steps that scientists use to answer questions and solve problems is often called the **scientific method.** The scientific method is not a rigid procedure. Scientists may use all of the steps or just some of the steps of the scientific method. They may even repeat some of the steps. The goal of the scientific method is to come up with reliable answers and solutions.

Six Steps of the Scientific Method

1 Ask a Question Good questions come from careful **observations.** You make observations by using your senses to gather information. Sometimes you may use instruments, such as microscopes and telescopes, to extend the range of your senses. As you observe the natural world, you will discover that you have many more questions than answers. These questions drive the scientific method.

Questions beginning with *what, why, how,* and *when* are very important in focusing an investigation, and they often lead to a hypothesis. (You will learn what a hypothesis is in the next step.) Here is an example of a question that could lead to further investigation.

Question: How does acid rain affect plant growth?

2 Form a Hypothesis After you come up with a question, you need to turn the question into a **hypothesis.** A hypothesis is a clear statement of what you expect the answer to your question to be. Your hypothesis will represent your best "educated guess" based on your observations and what you already know. A good hypothesis is testable. If observations and information cannot be gathered or if an experiment cannot be designed to test your hypothesis, it is untestable, and the investigation can go no further.

Here is a hypothesis that could be formed from the question, "How does acid rain affect plant growth?"

Hypothesis: Acid rain causes plants to grow more slowly.

Notice that the hypothesis provides some specifics that lead to methods of testing. The hypothesis can also lead to predictions. A **prediction** is what you think will be the outcome of your experiment or data collection. Predictions are usually stated in an "if . . . then" format. For example, **if** meat is kept at room temperature, **then** it will spoil faster than meat kept in the refrigerator. More than one prediction can be made for a single hypothesis. Here is a sample prediction for the hypothesis that acid rain causes plants to grow more slowly.

Prediction: If a plant is watered with only acid rain (which has a pH of 4), then the plant will grow at half its normal rate.

3 **Test the Hypothesis** After you have formed a hypothesis and made a prediction, you should test your hypothesis. There are different ways to do this. Perhaps the most familiar way is to conduct a **controlled experiment.** A controlled experiment tests only one factor at a time. A controlled experiment has a **control group** and one or more **experimental groups.** All the factors for the control and experimental groups are the same except for one factor, which is called the **variable.** By changing only one factor, you can see the results of just that one change.

Sometimes, the nature of an investigation makes a controlled experiment impossible. For example, dinosaurs have been extinct for millions of years, and the Earth's core is surrounded by thousands of meters of rock. It would be difficult, if not impossible, to conduct controlled experiments on such things. Under such circumstances, a hypothesis may be tested by making detailed observations. Taking measurements is one way of making observations.

Test the Hypothesis

4 **Analyze the Results** After you have completed your experiments, made your observations, and collected your data, you must analyze all the information you have gathered. Tables and graphs are often used in this step to organize the data.

Analyze the Results

5 **Draw Conclusions** Based on the analysis of your data, you should conclude whether or not your results support your hypothesis. If your hypothesis is supported, you (or others) might want to repeat the observations or experiments to verify your results. If your hypothesis is not supported by the data, you may have to check your procedure for errors. You may even have to reject your hypothesis and make a new one. If you cannot draw a conclusion from your results, you may have to try the investigation again or carry out further observations or experiments.

Draw Conclusions

Do they support your hypothesis?

No

Yes

6 **Communicate Results** After any scientific investigation, you should report your results. By doing a written or oral report, you let others know what you have learned. They may want to repeat your investigation to see if they get the same results. Your report may even lead to another question, which in turn may lead to another investigation.

Communicate Results

Scientific Method in Action

The scientific method is not a "straight line" of steps. It contains loops in which several steps may be repeated over and over again, while others may not be necessary. For example, sometimes scientists will find that testing one hypothesis raises new questions and new hypotheses to be tested. And sometimes, testing the hypothesis leads directly to a conclusion. Furthermore, the steps in the scientific method are not always used in the same order. Follow the steps in the diagram below, and see how many different directions the scientific method can take you.

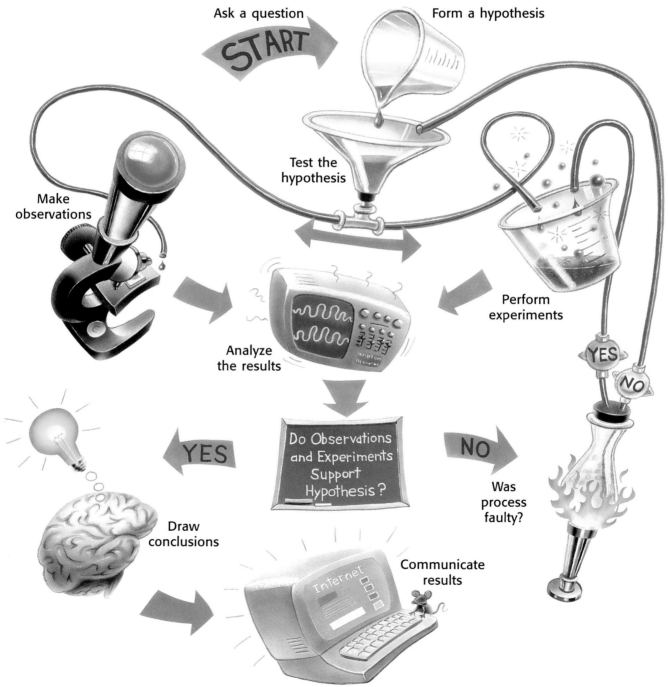

Ask a question

START

Form a hypothesis

Test the hypothesis

Make observations

Perform experiments

Analyze the results

YES

NO

YES

Do Observations and Experiments Support Hypothesis?

NO

Was process faulty?

Draw conclusions

Communicate results

Internet

Making Charts and Graphs

Circle Graphs

A circle graph, or pie chart, shows how each group of data relates to all of the data. Each part of the circle represents a category of the data. The entire circle represents all of the data. For example, a biologist studying a hardwood forest in Wisconsin found that there were five different types of trees. The data table at right summarizes the biologist's findings.

Wisconsin Hardwood Trees	
Type of tree	**Number found**
Oak	600
Maple	750
Beech	300
Birch	1,200
Hickory	150
Total	3,000

How to Make a Circle Graph

1 In order to make a circle graph of this data, first find the percentage of each type of tree. To do this, divide the number of individual trees by the total number of trees and multiply by 100.

$$\frac{600 \text{ oak}}{3{,}000 \text{ trees}} \times 100 = 20\%$$

$$\frac{750 \text{ maple}}{3{,}000 \text{ trees}} \times 100 = 25\%$$

$$\frac{300 \text{ beech}}{3{,}000 \text{ trees}} \times 100 = 10\%$$

$$\frac{1{,}200 \text{ birch}}{3{,}000 \text{ trees}} \times 100 = 40\%$$

$$\frac{150 \text{ hickory}}{3{,}000 \text{ trees}} \times 100 = 5\%$$

2 Now determine the size of the pie shapes that make up the chart. Do this by multiplying each percentage by 360°. Remember that a circle contains 360°.

$20\% \times 360° = 72°$ $25\% \times 360° = 90°$
$10\% \times 360° = 36°$ $40\% \times 360° = 144°$
$5\% \times 360° = 18°$

3 Then check that the sum of the percentages is 100 and the sum of the degrees is 360.

$20\% + 25\% + 10\% + 40\% + 5\% = 100\%$
$72° + 90° + 36° + 144° + 18° = 360°$

4 Use a compass to draw a circle and mark its center.

5 Then use a protractor to draw angles of 72°, 90°, 36°, 144°, and 18° in the circle.

6 Finally, label each part of the graph, and choose an appropriate title.

A Community of Wisconsin Hardwood Trees

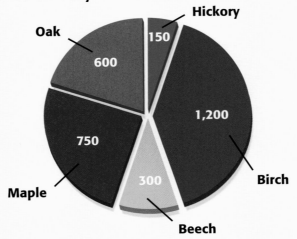

Line Graphs

Line graphs are most often used to demonstrate continuous change. For example, Mr. Smith's science class analyzed the population records for their hometown, Appleton, between 1900 and 2000. Examine the data at left.

Because the year and the population change, they are the *variables*. The population is determined by, or dependent on, the year. Therefore, the population is called the **dependent variable**, and the year is called the **independent variable**. Each set of data is called a **data pair**. To prepare a line graph, data pairs must first be organized in a table like the one at left.

Population of Appleton, 1900–2000	
Year	Population
1900	1,800
1920	2,500
1940	3,200
1960	3,900
1980	4,600
2000	5,300

How to Make a Line Graph

1 Place the independent variable along the horizontal (*x*) axis. Place the dependent variable along the vertical (*y*) axis.

2 Label the *x*-axis "Year" and the *y*-axis "Population." Look at your largest and smallest values for the population. Determine a scale for the *y*-axis that will provide enough space to show these values. You must use the same scale for the entire length of the axis. Find an appropriate scale for the *x*-axis too.

3 Choose reasonable starting points for each axis.

4 Plot the data pairs as accurately as possible.

5 Choose a title that accurately represents the data.

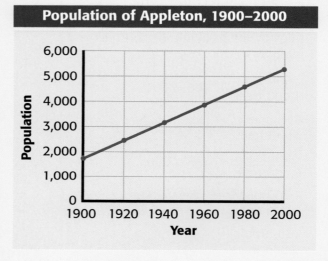

How to Determine Slope

Slope is the ratio of the change in the *y*-axis to the change in the *x*-axis, or "rise over run."

1 Choose two points on the line graph. For example, the population of Appleton in 2000 was 5,300 people. Therefore, you can define point *a* as (2000, 5,300). In 1900, the population was 1,800 people. Define point *b* as (1900, 1,800).

2 Find the change in the *y*-axis.
(*y* at point *a*) − (*y* at point *b*)
5,300 people − 1,800 people = 3,500 people

3 Find the change in the *x*-axis.
(*x* at point *a*) − (*x* at point *b*)
2000 − 1900 = 100 years

4 Calculate the slope of the graph by dividing the change in *y* by the change in *x*.

$$\text{slope} = \frac{\text{change in } y}{\text{change in } x}$$

$$\text{slope} = \frac{3,500 \text{ people}}{100 \text{ years}}$$

slope = 35 people per year

In this example, the population in Appleton increased by a fixed amount each year. The graph of this data is a straight line. Therefore, the relationship is **linear.** When the graph of a set of data is not a straight line, the relationship is **nonlinear.**

Using Algebra to Determine Slope

The equation in step 4 may also be arranged to be:

$$y = kx$$

where y represents the change in the y-axis, k represents the slope, and x represents the change in the x-axis.

$$\text{slope} = \frac{\text{change in } y}{\text{change in } x}$$

$$k = \frac{y}{x}$$

$$k \times x = \frac{y \times x}{x}$$

$$kx = y$$

Bar Graphs

Bar graphs are used to demonstrate change that is not continuous. These graphs can be used to indicate trends when the data are taken over a long period of time. A meteorologist gathered the precipitation records at right for Hartford, Connecticut, for April 1–15, 1996, and used a bar graph to represent the data.

Precipitation in Hartford, Connecticut April 1–15, 1996			
Date	Precipitation (cm)	Date	Precipitation (cm)
April 1	0.5	April 9	0.25
April 2	1.25	April 10	0.0
April 3	0.0	April 11	1.0
April 4	0.0	April 12	0.0
April 5	0.0	April 13	0.25
April 6	0.0	April 14	0.0
April 7	0.0	April 15	6.50
April 8	1.75		

How to Make a Bar Graph

❶ Use an appropriate scale and a reasonable starting point for each axis.

❷ Label the axes, and plot the data.

❸ Choose a title that accurately represents the data.

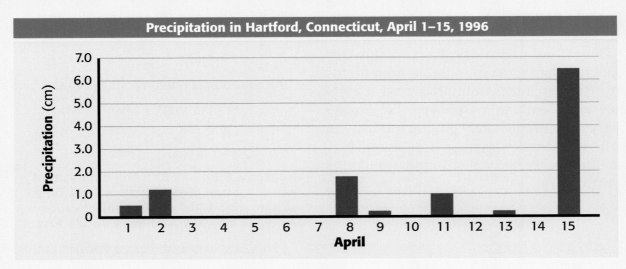

Precipitation in Hartford, Connecticut, April 1–15, 1996

Physical Science Laws and Principles

Law of Conservation of Energy

The law of conservation of energy states that energy can be neither created nor destroyed.

The total amount of energy in a closed system is always the same. Energy can be changed from one form to another, but all the different forms of energy in a system always add up to the same total amount of energy, no matter how many energy conversions occur.

Law of Universal Gravitation

The law of universal gravitation states that all objects in the universe attract each other by a force called gravity. The size of the force depends on the masses of the objects and the distance between them.

The first part of the law explains why a bowling ball is much harder to lift than a table-tennis ball. Because the bowling ball has a much larger mass than the table-tennis ball, the amount of gravity between the Earth and the bowling ball is greater than the amount of gravity between the Earth and the table-tennis ball.

The second part of the law explains why a satellite can remain in orbit around the Earth. The satellite is carefully placed at a distance great enough to prevent the Earth's gravity from immediately pulling it down but small enough to prevent it from completely escaping the Earth's gravity and wandering off into space.

Newton's Laws of Motion

Newton's first law of motion states that an object at rest remains at rest and an object in motion remains in motion at constant speed and in a straight line unless acted on by an unbalanced force.

The first part of the law explains why a football will remain on a tee until it is kicked off or until a gust of wind blows it off.

The second part of the law explains why a bike's rider will continue moving forward after the bike tire runs into a crack in the sidewalk and the bike comes to an abrupt stop until gravity and the sidewalk stop the rider.

Newton's second law of motion states that the acceleration of an object depends on the mass of the object and the amount of force applied.

The first part of the law explains why the acceleration of a 4 kg bowling ball will be greater than the acceleration of a 6 kg bowling ball if the same force is applied to both.

The second part of the law explains why the acceleration of a bowling ball will be larger if a larger force is applied to it.

The relationship of acceleration (a) to mass (m) and force (F) can be expressed mathematically by the following equation:

$$\text{acceleration} = \frac{\text{force}}{\text{mass}}, \text{ or } a = \frac{F}{m}$$

This equation is often rearranged to the form:

$$\text{force} = \text{mass} \times \text{acceleration},$$
$$\text{or}$$
$$F = m \times a$$

Newton's third law of motion states that whenever one object exerts a force on a second object, the second object exerts an equal and opposite force on the first.

This law explains that a runner is able to move forward because of the equal and opposite force the ground exerts on the runner's foot after each step.

Law of Reflection

The law of reflection states that the angle of incidence is equal to the angle of reflection. This law explains why light reflects off of a surface at the same angle it strikes the surface.

A line perpendicular to the mirror's surface is called the *normal*.

The beam of light reflected off the mirror is called the *reflected beam*.

The beam of light traveling toward the mirror is called the *incident beam*.

The angle between the incident beam and the normal is called the *angle of incidence*.

The angle between the reflected beam and the normal is called the *angle of reflection*.

Charles's Law

Charles's law states that for a fixed amount of gas at a constant pressure, the volume of the gas increases as its temperature increases. Likewise, the volume of the gas decreases as its temperature decreases.

If a basketball that was inflated indoors is left outside on a cold winter day, the air particles inside of the ball will move more slowly. They will hit the sides of the basketball less often and with less force. The ball will get smaller as the volume of the air decreases. If a basketball that was inflated outdoors on a cold winter day is brought indoors, the air particles inside of the ball will move more rapidly. They will hit the sides of the basketball more often and with more force. The ball will get larger as the volume of the air increases.

Boyle's Law

Boyle's law states that for a fixed amount of gas at a constant temperature, the volume of a gas increases as its pressure decreases. Likewise, the volume of a gas decreases as its pressure increases.

This law explains why the pressure of the gas in a helium balloon decreases as the balloon rises from the Earth's surface.

Pascal's Principle

Pascal's principle states that a change in pressure at any point in an enclosed fluid will be transmitted equally to all parts of that fluid.

When a mechanic uses a hydraulic jack to raise an automobile off the ground, he or she increases the pressure on the fluid in the jack by pushing on the jack handle. The pressure is transmitted equally to all parts of the fluid-filled jacking system. The fluid presses the jack plate against the frame of the car, lifting the car off the ground.

Archimedes' Principle

Archimedes' principle states that the buoyant force on an object in a fluid is equal to the weight of the volume of fluid that the object displaces.

A person floating in a swimming pool displaces 20 L of water. The weight of that volume of water is about 200 N. Therefore, the buoyant force on the person is 200 N.

Glossary

A

absorption the transfer of energy carried by light waves to particles of matter (74)

amplitude the maximum distance a wave vibrates from its rest position (10, 39)

Archimedes' (ahr kuh MEE deez) **principle** the principle that states that the buoyant force on an object in a fluid is an upward force equal to the weight of the volume of fluid that the object displaces (145)

B

Boyle's law the law that states that for a fixed amount of gas at a constant temperature, the volume of a gas increases as its pressure decreases (145)

C

Charles's law the law that states that for a fixed amount of gas at a constant pressure, the volume of a gas increases as its temperature increases (145)

compression a region of higher density or pressure in a wave (8, 30)

concave lens a lens that is thinner in the middle than at the edges (104)

concave mirror a mirror that is curved inward like the inside of a spoon (100)

constructive interference interference that results in a wave that has a greater amplitude than that of the individual waves (17, 44, 77)

convex lens a lens that is thicker in the middle than at the edges (103)

convex mirror a mirror that is curved outward like the back of a spoon (102)

cornea a transparent membrane that protects the eye and refracts light (105)

crest the highest point of a transverse wave (7)

D

decibel (dB) the most common unit used to express loudness (39)

destructive interference interference that results in a wave that has a smaller amplitude than that of the individual waves (17, 44, 77)

diffraction

diffraction the bending of waves around a barrier or through an opening (15, 47, 77)

Doppler effect the apparent change in the frequency of a sound caused by the motion of either the listener or the source of the sound (refers to sound only) (38)

E

echo a reflected sound wave (14, 41)

echolocation the process of using reflected sound waves to find objects (42)

electromagnetic spectrum the entire range of electromagnetic waves (65)

electromagnetic wave a wave that can travel through space or matter and consists of changing electric and magnetic fields (6, 62)

F

fiber optics the use of optical fibers (thin, flexible glass wires) to transmit light over long distances (112)

fluorescent light visible light emitted by a phosphor particle when it absorbs energy such as ultraviolet light (96)

focal length the distance between a mirror or lens and its focal point (100)

focal point the point on the axis of a mirror or lens through which all incident parallel light rays are focused (100)

frequency the number of waves produced in a given amount of time (12, 36)

fundamental the lowest resonant frequency (46)

G

gamma rays EM waves with very high energy and no mass or charge; they are emitted by the nucleus of a radioactive atom (72)

H

hertz (Hz) the unit used to express frequency; one hertz is one cycle per second (12, 36)

hologram a piece of film on which an interference pattern produces a three-dimensional image of an object (111)

I

illuminated the term describing visible objects that are not a light source (94)

incandescent light light produced by hot objects (95)

infrared waves EM waves that are between microwaves and visible light in the electromagnetic spectrum (69)

infrasonic the term describing sounds with frequencies lower than 20 Hz (37)

inner ear the part of the ear where vibrations created by sound are changed into electrical signals for the brain to interpret (33)

interference a wave interaction that occurs when two or more waves overlap (16, 44, 77)

iris the colored part of the eye (105)

L

laser a device that produces intense light of only one wavelength and color (109)

law of reflection the law that states that the angle of incidence is equal to the angle of reflection (73)

lens a curved, transparent object that forms an image by refracting light (103); *also* the part of the eye that refracts light to focus an image on the retina (105)

longitudinal wave a wave in which the particles of the medium vibrate back and forth along the path that the wave travels (8)

loudness how loud or soft a sound is perceived to be (38)

luminous the term describing objects that produce visible light (94)

M

medium a substance through which a wave can travel (5, 32)

microwaves EM waves that are between radio waves and infrared waves in the electromagnetic spectrum (68)

middle ear the part of the ear where the amplitude of sound vibrations is increased (33)

N

neon light light emitted by atoms of certain gases, such as neon, when they absorb and then release energy (96)

noise any undesired sound, especially nonmusical sound, that includes a random mix of pitches (51)

O

opaque the term describing matter that does not transmit any light (80)

optical axis a straight line drawn outward from the center of a mirror or lens (100)

oscilloscope (uh SIL uh SKOHP) a device used to graph representations of sound waves (40)

outer ear the part of the ear that acts as a funnel to direct sound waves into the middle ear (33)

overtones resonant frequencies that are higher than the fundamental (46)

P

Pascal's principle the principle that states that a change in pressure at any point in an enclosed fluid is transmitted equally to all parts of that fluid (145)

perpendicular at right angles (7, 62)

photon a tiny "packet" of energy that is released by an electron that moves to a lower energy level in an atom (63)

pigment a material that gives a substance its color by absorbing some colors of light and reflecting others (82)

pitch how high or low a sound is perceived to be (36)

plane mirror a mirror with a flat surface (99)

polarized light consists of light waves that vibrate in only one plane (one direction) (112)

primary colors of light red, blue, and green; these colors of light can be combined in different ratios to produce all colors of light (82)

primary pigments yellow, cyan, and magenta; these pigments can be combined to produce any other pigment (83)

pupil the opening to the inside of the eye (105)

R

radiation the transfer of energy through matter or space as electromagnetic waves, such as visible light and infrared waves (63)

radio waves EM waves with long wavelengths and low frequencies (66)

rarefaction (RER uh FAK shuhn) a region of lower density or pressure in a wave (8, 30)

real image an image through which light passes (100)

reflection the bouncing back of a wave after it strikes a barrier or an object (14, 41, 73)

refraction the bending of a wave as it passes at an angle from one medium to another (15, 75)

resonance what occurs when an object vibrating at or near a resonant frequency of a second object causes the second object to vibrate (18, 46)

resonant frequencies the frequencies at which standing waves are made (18, 46)

retina the back surface of the eye (105)

S

scattering the release of light energy by particles of matter that have absorbed energy (75)

secondary color cyan, magenta, and yellow; a color of light produced when two primary colors of light are added together (82)

sonar (**so**und **na**vigation and **r**anging) a type of electronic echolocation (42)

sonic boom the explosive sound heard when a shock wave from an object traveling faster than the speed of sound reaches a person's ears (45)

sound quality the result of several pitches blending together through interference (48)

standing wave a wave that forms a stationary pattern in which portions of the wave do not move and other portions move with a large amplitude (18, 45)

surface wave a wave that occurs at or near the boundary of two media and that is a combination of transverse and longitudinal waves (9)

T

tinnitus hearing loss resulting from damage to the hair cells and nerve endings in the cochlea (34)

translucent the term describing matter that transmits light but also scatters the light as it passes through the matter (80)

transmission the passing of light through matter (79)

transparent the term describing matter through which light is easily transmitted (80)

transverse wave a wave in which the particles of the wave's medium vibrate perpendicular to the direction the wave is traveling (7)

trough the lowest point of a transverse wave (7)

U

ultrasonic the term describing sounds with frequencies higher than 20,000 Hz (37)

ultrasonography a medical procedure that uses echoes from ultrasonic waves to "see" inside a patient's body without performing surgery (43)

ultraviolet light EM waves that are between visible light and X rays in the electromagnetic spectrum (71)

V

vapor light light produced when electrons combine with gaseous metal atoms (97)

vibration the complete back-and-forth motion of an object (30)

virtual image an image through which light does not actually pass (99)

visible light the very narrow range of wavelengths and frequencies in the electromagnetic spectrum that humans can see (70)

W

wave a disturbance that transmits energy through matter or space (4, 31)

wavelength the distance between one point on a wave and the corresponding point on an adjacent wave in a series of waves (11)

wave speed the speed at which a wave travels (13)

X

X rays high-energy EM waves that are between ultraviolet light and gamma rays in the electromagnetic spectrum (72)

Index

A **boldface** number refers to an illustration on that page.

A

absorption, **74,** 74–75
amplitude, **10,** 10–11
    of sound waves, 38–40, **40**
amplitude modulation, 66–67, **67**
angle of incidence, 73, **73,** 145
angle of reflection, 73, **73, 74,** 145
azurite, 83

B

bar graphs, 143, **143**
beluga whales, 41, **41**
booming sands, 38

C

cameras, 108, **108**
cars, side mirrors, 102
chlorophyll, 83
color, **70,** 75–76, **76,** 80–83, **82,**
    83. See also light
    mixing of, **82,** 82–83, **83**
    of objects, 80–81, **81**
    separation, 76, **76**
color deficiency, 107, **107**
compression, 8, **8, 30, 31**
concave lenses, 104, **104, 106**
concave mirrors, **100,** 100–101, **101**
constructive interference, **17,**
    17–18, **18,** 77, **78**
convex lenses, **103,** 103–104, **106**
convex mirrors, 102, **102**
cornea, 105, **105**
crest, 7

D

deafness, 34
decibels, 39
destructive interference, 17, **17, 18,**
    78, **78**
Diegert, Carl, 58
diffraction, 15–16, **16,** 47, **47,** 77, **77**
diffuse reflection, 74, **74**
dinosaurs, 58
Doppler effect, 38, **38**
drums, 50, **50**

E

E. coli, 90
ears, **33,** 59. See also hearing
earthquakes, 9
echoes, 14, 41, **41**
echolocation, **42,** 42–43
Einstein, Albert, 63, **63**
electromagnetic spectrum, 65–72,
    66–67. See also light
electromagnetic wave, 62, **62**

electromagnetism
    light waves, **62,** 62–63, 65
elephants, 27, **27**
energy, in waves, 4–6, 11–12
Escherichia coli, 90
eyes, **105,** 105–107, **106**

F

farsightedness, 106, **106**
fiber optics, 112
fields
    electromagnetic waves and, 62
fireflies, 90
fluorescence, 116, 119
fluorescent light, 96, **96**
focal length, **100, 101**
focal point, **100, 102, 103**
frequency, 12
    of light, 65–72
    of sound, 36–37, **37**
frequency modulation, 66–67, **67**

G

gamma rays, 67, **67,** 72
gas masks, 120

H

halogen lights, 95, **95**
headphones, **34**
health
    food contamination, 90
    hearing problems, 34, 51
    kidney stones, 37
    radiation in medicine, 72
    ultrasound, 43, **43**
    vision problems, **106,** 106–107,
    107
    vitamin D, 71
    X rays, 72, **72**
hearing, **33,** 34, 37, **37,** 51
hertz, 12
holograms, 111, **111**

I

illuminated objects, 94. See also
    light
incandescent light, 95, **95**
incidence, angle of, 73, 145
infrared waves, **66,** 69, **69**
infrasonic frequencies, 27, 37
infrasound, 27
inner ear, **33**
interference, **16,** 16–19, **44,** 44–46,
    77–78, **78**
iris, **105**

K

kidney stones, 37

L

lasers,
    in holograms, 111, **111**
    operation of, 109–110, **110**
law of reflection, 73, **73,** 144
lenses, **103,** 103–104, **104, 105,**
    106, 108
light. See also lasers; light bulbs;
    waves
    absorption and scattering, **74,**
    74–75
    coherent, 109
    colors, **70,** 75–76, **76,** 79–82, **82**
    diffraction, 77, **77**
    fiber optics, 112
    fluorescent, 96, **96**
    frequencies of, 65–72
    infrared, **66,** 69, **69**
    matter and, 79–80
    neon, 96, **96**
    optical instruments, **108,**
    108–109, **109**
    polarized, 112–113, **113**
    pollution, 121
    production of, 63
    rays, 98, **98,** 100
    sight and, 73, **105,** 105–107, **106**
    speed of, 64, 65, **75**
    transmission of, 79
    ultraviolet, **67,** 71
    visible, **67,** 70
    waves, 6, **15,** 62, 65–72
light bulbs
    types of, **95, 96,** 96–97, **97**
lightning, 47, **64**
longitudinal waves, **8,** 8–9, **11,** 31,
    31
loudness, 38–40
luminous objects, 94, 116. See also
    light

M

magnetrons, 91
magnets, 62
magnifying glasses, **103**
malachite, 83
marimba, **18**
matter, light and, 79–80
medium, 5, 75
    sound and, 32, 35–36
microscopes, 109
microwave ovens, **68,** 91
microwaves, **66,** 68–69
middle ear, **33**
mirrors, **99,** 99–102, **100, 101, 102**
modulation of radio waves, 66–67,
    67, 68
Morgan, Garrett, 120
music, 51, **51**
musical instruments, **48,** 48–50,
    49, 50

Credits

Abbreviations used: (t) top, (c) center, (b) bottom, (l) left, (r) right, (bkgd) background

ILLUSTRATIONS

All illustrations, unless noted below, by Holt, Rinehart and Winston.

Table of Contents v, Gary Ferster; vii, Sidney Jablonski.

Chapter One Page 4, Will Nelson/Sweet Reps; 7(tr), Preface, Inc.; 7(b), 8(t,c), John White/The Neis Group; 8(b), Sidney Jablonski; 9(tl), Stephen Durke/Washington Artists; 9(r), Jared Schneidman/Wilkinson Studios; 10(t), Marty Roper/Planet Rep; 10(b), 11, 12, Sidney Jablonski; 12(cl, cr), 13(cl,cr), Mike Carroll/Steve Edsey & Sons; 13, 15, Will Nelson/Sweet Reps; 17(tl,tc,tr,cl,c,cr), John White/The Neis Group; 17(br), Terry Guyer; 22(b), John White/The Neis Group; 25(r), Sidney Jablonski.

Chapter Two Page 30, Annie Bissett; 31(l), Gary Ferster; 31(br), Terry Kovalcik; 32(tl), David Merrell/Suzanne Craig, 33, Keith Kasnot; 34 (tl), Terry Kovalcik; 35, Keith Locke/Suzanne Craig; 36, Annie Bissett; 37, Will Nelson/ Sweet Reps (dolphin, cat, dog), Rob Wood (whale), Michael Woods (bat, bird), John White/ The Neis Group (girl), and Preface, Inc.; 38, Gary Ferster; 40, Annie Bissett; 41(b), John White/The Neis Group; 42(t), Gary Ferster; 42(b), Terry Guyer; 44(t), Gary Ferster; 44(b), 45, Terry Guyer; 47, 48(c), Gary Ferster; 48(b), 51, Annie Bissett; 54(br), Keith Kasnot; 57(r), Annie Bissett; 58, Barbara Hoopes-Ambler.

Chapter Three Page 62, Sidney Jablonski; 63(tr), Blake Thornton/Rita Marie; 63(b), Stephen Durke/Washington Artists; 66(t), Blake Thornton/Rita Marie; 66(b), Preface, Inc.; 67(tl,tr), Terry Guyer; 67 (b), Preface, Inc.; 68, Dan Stuckenschneider/Uhl Studios Inc.; 70, Preface, Inc.; 71, Blake Thornton/Rita Marie; 72, 73, 74, Dan Stuckenschneider/Uhl Studios Inc.; 76, Stephen Durke/ Washington Artists; 78, Preface, Inc.; 80, Dave Joly; 81, Preface, Inc.; 86, Stephen Durke/Washington Artists.

Chapter Four Page 95, 96, 97, Dan Stuckenschneider/Uhl Studios Inc.; 98, Stephen Durke/Washington Artists; 99, Preface, Inc.; 101, 102, 103, 104, Will Nelson/Sweet Reps (flowers) and Preface, Inc.; 105, Keith Kasnot; 106, Keith Kasnot and Preface Inc.; 108, 109, Dan Stuckenschneider/Uhl Studios Inc.; 110(t), Digital Art; 110(b), Stephen Durke/Washington Artists; 111, Digital Art; 112, Stephen Durke/ Washington Artists; 116(t), Dan Stuckenschneider/Uhl Studios Inc.; 116(b), Keith Kasnot; 119, Stephen Durke/Washington Artists (rulers) and Preface, Inc.

LabBook Page 130, Blake Thornton/Rita Marie; 132, Terry Guyer; 134, John White/The Neis Group.

Appendix Page 140(b), Mark Mille/Sharon Langley Artist Rep.; 141, 142, 143, Preface, Inc.; 145(t), Dan Stuckenschneider/Uhl Studios Inc.

PHOTOGRAPHY

Front Cover and Title Page: Telegraph Colour Library/FPG

Table of Contents Page v(tr), Richard Megna/Fundamental Photographs; v(b), Sam Dudgeon/HRW Photo; vi(t), Richard Megna/Fundamental Photographs; vi(c), Matt Meadows/Photo Researchers, Inc.; vi(b), Robert Wolf; vii(t), James L. Amos/National Geographic Society; vii(c), Dr. E.R. Degginger/ColorPic, Inc.; vii(b), John Langford/HRW Photo.

Feature Borders Unless otherwise noted below, all images ©2001 PhotoDisc/HRW: "Across the Sciences" 27, all images by HRW; "Eureka" 91, ©2001 PhotoDisc/HRW; "Eye on the Environment" 121, clouds and sea in bkgd, HRW, bkgd grass and red eyed frog, Corbis Images, hawks and pelican, Animals Animals/Earth Scenes, rat, John Grelach/Visuals Unlimited, endangered flower, Dan Suzio/Photo Researchers, Inc.; "Science Fiction" 59, saucers, Ian Christopher/Greg Geisler, book, HRW, bkgd, Stock Illustration Source; "Science, Technology, and Society" 26, 58, 90, 120, robot, Greg Geisler.

Chapter One pp. 2-3 Jim Russi/Adventure Photo; p. 3 HRW Photo; p. 5(t), Phil Degginger/Color-Pic, Inc.; p. 5(b), Emil Muench/Photo Researchers, Inc.; p. 6, Norbert Wu; p. 14(b), Erich Schrempp/Photo Researchers, Inc. ; p. 14, Don Spiro/Stone; p. 16(tl,tr,), Richard Megna/Fundamental Photographs; p. 16(b), Richard Hamilton Smith/Corbis-Bettmann; p. 18(t), Richard Megna/ Fundamental Photographs; p. 19, AP/Wide World Photos; p. 21 Sam Dudgeon/HRW Photo; p. 22, Norbert Wu; p. 24, Richard Megna/Fundamental Photographs; p. 25, Martin Bough/Fundamental Photographs; p. 26, Pete Saloutos/The Stock Market; p. 27, Betty K. Bruce/Animals Animals/Earth Scenes.

Chapter Two pp. 28-29 Kim Westerskov/Stone; p. 29 HRW Photo; p. 34(c), Michael A. Keller/The Picture Cube; p. 39(cl), Art Wolfe/ Stone; p. 39(b), Tom Hannon/Picture Cube; p. 40, Charles D. Winters/Timeframe Photography Inc.; p. 41, Dr. E.R. Degginger/Color-Pic, Inc.; p. 42, Stephen Dalton/Photo Researchers, Inc.; p. 43(b), Matt Meadows/Photo Researchers, Inc.; p. 43(t), courtesy of Johann Borenstein; p. 46(b,c), Richard Megna/ Fundamental Photographs; p. 49(l), p. 50 (tl,tr), Image Club Graphics © 1998 Adobe Systems; p. 50(br), Bob Daemmrich/HRW Photo; p. 53 Sam Dudgeon/HRW Photo; p. 56, Ross Harrison Koty/Stone; p. 57, Dick Luria/Photo Researchers, Inc.

Chapter Three pp. 60-61 Matt Meadows/Peter Arnold, Inc.; p. 61 HRW Photo; p. 63, Photo Researchers, Inc.; p. 64, A.T. Willet/The Image Bank; p. 65(r,l), Leonard Lessing/Photo Researchers, Inc.; p. 65(c), Michael Fogden and Patricia Fogden/Corbis; p. 66(l), Robert Wolf; p. 67(c), Hugh Turvey/Science Photo Library/Photo Researchers, Inc.; p. 67(r), Blair Seitz/Photo Researchers, Inc.; p. 67(l), Leonide Principe/Photo Researchers, Inc.; p. 69(t), Bachmann/ Photo Researchers, Inc.; p. 69(b), The Stock Market; p. 70, Cameron Davidson/Stone; p. 72, Michael English/Custom Medical Stock Photo; p. 75, Richard Megna/Fundamental Photographs; p. 76, Robert Wolf; p. 77(t), Fundamental Photographs; p. 79(t), Robert Wolf; p. 79(b), Stephanie Morris/ HRW Photo; p. 81(t), Image copyright 2001 PhotoDisc, Inc.; p. 81(c), Renee Lynn/Davis/Lynn Images; p. 81(b), Robert Wolf; p. 82, Leonard Lessing/Peter Arnold, Inc.; p. 83, Index Stock Photography; p. 85 Sam Dudgeon/HRW Photo; p. 86, Leonard Lessing/ Photo Researchers, Inc.; p. 87, Robert Wolf; p. 89(tr), Charles Winters/Photo Researchers, Inc.; p. 89(cr), Mark E. Gibson; p. 89(br), Richard Megna/Fundamental Photographs; p. 90(t,b), Dr. E.R. Degginger/ Color-Pic, Inc.; p. 91, courtesy of the Raytheon Company.

Chapter Four pp. 92-93 The Purcell Team/CORBIS; p. 93 HRW Photo; p. 94 (b), Harry Rogers/Photo Researchers, Inc.; p. 94(r), Kindra Clinett/The Picture Cube; p. 96, Peter Van Steen/HRW Photo; p. 97, Alan Schein/The Stock Market; p. 98(tr), Yoav Levy/Phototake; p. 99(tr), Stephanie Morris/HRW Photo; p. 100(c), Richard Megna/Fundamental Photographs; p. 102, p. 103(b), Robert Wolf; p. 103(t,c), Dr. E.R. Degginger/Color-Pic, Inc.; p. 107(l,r), Leonard Lessing/Peter Arnold, Inc.; p. 112, Don Mason/The Stock Market; p. 113(l,r), Ken Lax; p. 114 Sam Dudgeon/HRW Photo; p. 118, James L. Amos/National Geographic Society; p. 120(b), US Patent and Trade Office; p. 120(t), Private collection of Garrett Morgan Family; p. 121(b), NASA; p. 121(t), SuperStock.

LabBook "LabBook Header": "L," Corbis Images, "a," Letraset Phototone, "b" and "B," HRW, "o" and "k," Images ©2001 PhotoDisc/HRW; 123(c), Michelle Bridwell/HRW Photo; 123(br), Image © 2001 PhotoDisc, Inc.; 124(cl), Victoria Smith/HRW Photo; 124(bl), Stephanie Morris/HRW Photo; 125(tl), Patti Murray/Animals Animals; 125(b), Peter Van Steen/HRW Photo; 125(tr), Jana Birchum/HRW Photo; 127, 128, Richard Megna/Fundamental Photographs.

Sam Dudgeon/HRW Photo Page viii-1; 12; 23; 31(b); 32; 34(r); 37(t); 46(t); 48; 54-55; 66(c); 88; 94(l); 100(b); 111; 122; 123(b); 124(br,t); 125(tl); 126; 129; 131; 133; 135.

John Langford/HRW Photo Page v(cr); vi(tr); 18(b); 31(t); 39(t,bc); 49(r); 66(r); 71; 74; 77(b); 80; 94(inset); 99(b); 100(tl); 101(b); 119; 123(t).

Scott Van Osdol/HRW Photo Page 89(bl).

Self-Check Answers

Chapter 1—The Energy of Waves

Page 6: Mechanical waves require a medium; electromagnetic waves do not.

Page 15: A light wave will not refract if it enters a new medium perpendicular to the surface because the entire wave enters the new medium at the same time.

Chapter 2—The Nature of Sound

Page 45: A person hears a sonic boom when a shock wave reaches his or her ears. If two people are standing a block or two apart, the shock wave will reach them at different times, so they will hear sonic booms at different times.

Page 49: Interference is the most important wave interaction for determining sound quality.

Chapter 3—The Nature of Light

Page 81: The paper will appear blue because only blue light is reflected from the paper.

Chapter 4—Light and Our World

Page 109: Concave lenses do not form real images. Only a real image can be magnified by another lens, such as the eyepiece lens.